Caring
for your
Church
Building

James
Halsall

**kevin
mayhew**

kevin
mayhew

First published in Great Britain in 2015 by Kevin Mayhew Ltd

Buxhall, Stowmarket, Suffolk IP14 3BW
Tel: +44 (0) 1449 737978 Fax: +44 (0) 1449 737834
E-mail: info@kevinmayhewltd.com

www.kevinmayhew.com

9 8 7 6 5 4 3 2 1 0

ISBN 978 1 84867 779 1
Catalogue No. 1501476

Cover design by Rob Mortonson
Edited by John Cox
Typeset by Chris Coe

Printed and bound in Great Britain

Contents

About the author

James Halsall was born in Bradford and attended Fulneck Moravian School. After a period working in the Middle East he returned to the city of his birth and worked for the Diocese of Bradford for ten years. In 1990 he moved to Suffolk into the Diocese of St Edmundsbury and Ipswich and in 1994 was appointed Secretary of the Diocesan Advisory Committee for the Care of Churches – a job he describes as the best in the world.

James has contributed essays on church buildings to *Faith Matters*[1] and an article on Anglo-Saxon carvings to *Masterpieces: Art and East Anglia*.[2] He lives with Marion near the Suffolk coast where they enjoy gardening and walking with Barley, their Golden Retriever.

---

1. *Faith Matters*, Edited by John Cox (Kevin Mayhew, 2013).
2. *Masterpieces: Art and East Anglia*, Edited by Ian Collins (UEA Sainsbury Centre for Visual Arts, 2013).

Foreword

The Church of England has responsibility for 16,000 parish churches, 12,500 of which are listed. Most of these are cared for by volunteers and others who have had no professional training in historic buildings and their conservation, which is why a book like this is so helpful.

James Halsall, one of the most experienced professionals supporting church buildings, both across the diocese of St Edmundsbury and Ipswich and the church nationally, has written an excellent accessible and comprehensive book on the subject.

He brings order to a complicated and multifaceted subject matter, for at the heart of the ecclesiastical planning system is getting the balance right between making buildings fit for mission and worship and community use while respecting their heritage.

This book will help us get that balance right and therefore be able to enjoy church buildings with all they have to offer, enabling them to be creatively used and handed on in good shape for the future.

Janet Gough
Director, Cathedral and Church
Buildings Division (ChurchCare)

Acknowledgements

Dedicated volunteers caring for our wonderful churches should never need to work in isolation. When planning a re-ordering scheme or a roof repair, there should always be advice and support available within PCCs or at diocesan level. I have personally been most fortunate in being able to receive advice and support from a range of people when writing this book.

I am grateful to Michael Archer, Ian Coote, John Cox, Nicholas Edgell, Mark Ellis, Pedro Gaspar, Janet Gough, James Hall, David Hawkins, Stuart Hobley, David Knight, John Moore, Ian Morrison, Alan Moult, Anne Sloman, Margaret Statham, Derrick Stiff and Martin Stuchfield. Marion, my wife, deserves special mention for the hours spent poring over my drafts, suggesting alterations and coping with far too many conversations that revolved round church buildings.

Introduction

Every square centimetre of England falls within an ecclesiastical parish. Medieval churches with sturdy towers, Victorian churches with soaring spires, city churches resolutely standing their ground against sky-high office blocks or comfortable no-nonsense buildings in towns and suburbs. Old or new, these buildings were created principally for one purpose and continue to deliver that role today, standing as a strong reminder of the ongoing Christian traditions of these islands.

Step into the nave of an historic church and you will soon be able to piece together a narrative of the worshipping community down the centuries. Seating is a good example. You might find ornate benches from the sixteenth century, Georgian box pews for the squire and his family, solid Victorian stalls for the choir, and functional twentieth century chairs in an aisle, all in the same building.

Medieval churches will have witnessed turbulent periods of history when clergy and worshippers feared for their lives over matters of liturgy and, for those who know where to look, it is the absence of objects that tell the most dramatic story. The deep cuts in the chancel arch showing where a rood screen once stood; the sawn-off beams in the roof where angels once looked down on the congregation, and the attempted erasing of the faces of saints on screens or fonts – all were attempts to sweep away devotional images under the charge of idolatry.

As we have seen, church buildings have been altered over time and must continue to evolve if they are to survive as active centres of mission and ministry. With so many legal niceties, the pace of change may seem snail-like compared with other aspects of our lives. Yet there is clearly a need to pass on the rich legacy we have inherited and the church is, after all, an important building for the whole community, regular worshippers or not.

Caring for church buildings is therefore a hugely responsible task, requiring a delicate balance between the need to adapt to meet the practical requirements/needs of both worshippers and the local community, while not sacrificing an irreplaceable chunk of the historic narrative.

This book is aimed at the remarkable people who undertake this demanding role on a voluntary basis. If you are one of them, I hope the following chapters will help to guide you through the process of change with clear signposts of whom to consult and where to seek help.

I make no claim to having the answers to the complex legal issues or technical architectural challenges you may encounter along the way. You will be able to consult experts, such as your diocesan registrar or architect, to help you with those matters. On the other hand, if you need to know the course of action for clearing a space of pews, what's included in a quinquennial inspection report, or what options there are for heating an historic building, then this book is for you.

I have spent 20 years as secretary of a Diocesan Advisory Committee, dealing with everything from shoe-horning an equal access WC into the confined space of a church tower, to relocating a medieval font to create a more useable space in the nave, and virtually everything in between.

While, for the sake of simplicity, the terminology throughout this book refers to Church of England processes, I hope readers from other Christian denominations will also find the book helpful, as many of our priorities are shared and the advice here should be relevant to all.

Author's note

The way in which the faculty jurisdiction system is operated across the country is changing. We are on the cusp of new and easier ways of obtaining consent to work on church buildings. During 2015, many dioceses will introduce an online faculty system which will allow PCCs to complete forms and submit applications electronically. Later in the year, two lists will be approved by the General Synod of the Church of England detailing work that can be undertaken without the need for a full faculty. Your DAC's webpages will pass on information regarding these changes as they develop. This book provides information on the current system and, where possible, looks to the future.

Chapter 1

Faculties and Permissions

Over 85 per cent[3] of Anglican churches are listed under legislation[4] as of national or international historical and architectural importance. Contrast this with the fact that nationwide only 2 per cent[5] of all buildings are listed, and you can't help but begin to see the importance of the Church of England's building stock as a major and much-loved component of this country's built heritage. Caring for this estate is vitally important, not only because churches are a key part of the nation's heritage, but crucially as centres of local worship and mission.

Like other major denominations, the Church of England is exempt[6] from a range of secular controls. The most notable exemption is from the need to obtain listed building consent for works to listed buildings used for 'ecclesiastical purposes'[7] (see Note 1). It hasn't always been so.

In the early twentieth century, the Government was concerned that the Church of England, like many owners of historic properties – notably large country houses – was not looking after its buildings as well as it should. It therefore planned to legislate.[8] At that point, the then Archbishop of Canterbury, Randall Davidson, waded in saying he was concerned about state control of churches and successfully argued that the Church could maintain its buildings by setting

3. Church of England.
4. The Planning (Listed Buildings and Conservation Areas) Act 1990.
5. English Heritage (Heritage at Risk report).
6. The Care of Churches and Ecclesiastical Exemption Measure 1991.
7. Planning (Listed Buildings and Conservation Areas) Act 1990 para 60 (1).
8. Ancient Monuments Consolidation and Amendment Act 1913.

up advisory groups of experts. His proposal won exemption from the Act and saw the emergence of ecclesiastical exemption managed by the faculty jurisdiction process.

Six other denominations have ecclesiastical exemption. They are the Church in Wales; the Roman Catholic Church; the Baptist Union of Great Britain; the Baptist Union of Wales; the Methodist Church; and the United Reformed Church.

While this book relates to Church of England processes, members of other 'exempt' denominations will find similarities with their own systems.

Faculty jurisdiction in the Church of England

All work on any church building requires the diocesan bishop's permission. That's the theory. In practice the granting of permission has been devolved to the diocesan chancellor, the principal legal officer in the diocese, who relies on the advice of local experts to determine whether permission should be granted. Each diocese has a diocesan advisory committee for the care of churches (shortened to DAC) and, as well as advising the chancellor, the DAC will be able to advise you and your parochial church council (PCC). The permission the chancellor gives is called a 'faculty' and work should not begin on a church until the chancellor has issued it.

The system of applying for a faculty is changing (see Note 2). Two lists will be published in late 2015/early 2016 that will provide you with categories of work you can undertake without recourse to the chancellor and the full faculty application process. List A will contain minor work that can be done without consulting anyone. List B will contain work that requires the authorisation of the archdeacon after consultation with the DAC but without the need for a faculty. Any work not contained in lists A or B needs a faculty. Ask your archdeacon or DAC secretary if in doubt.

Why the need for faculties?

The role of church buildings, listed or otherwise, is primarily for worship and mission and this has to take priority when considering changes, as the opening paragraph of the Care of Churches and Ecclesiastical Jurisdiction Measure 1991 makes clear:

'Any person or body carrying out functions of care and conservation under this Measure or under any other enactment or rule of law relating to churches shall have due regard to the role of a church as a local centre of worship and mission.'

So does this mean that, if our project will aid the mission of the church, we will automatically receive approval? I am afraid not. The system has to be rigorous since Ecclesiastical Exemption is something of a gift that the Government could revoke if it is not exercised with due diligence and care.

Where do we start? The faculty process

The process for applying for a faculty is explained in a flowchart in Appendix A. Sufficient time should be allowed for a 28-day period for the display of public notices outlining your proposals.

Ecclesiastical Exemption, as we have seen, allows exemption from listed building consent. Local authority planning permission is another matter and, in the case of churches, will always apply to proposed changes in the outside appearance of your building. You will still need a faculty as well and would be well advised to obtain this before applying for planning permission.

Everyone on board

A project to build an extension is perhaps one of the most ambitious changes you will make to your church building and it is dealt with in the chapter on Improvements (see page 41).

A church extension is a relatively ambitious project.

In this, as with other major changes, you can expect at least one site visit which, in most circumstances, your DAC Secretary will arrange (see Note 3). He/she will invite all interested parties to attend including, if applicable, the local authority. Interested parties might include English Heritage (known as Historic England as from 1 April 2015 and the name used throughout this book), the Church Buildings Council, and the relevant amenity societies. (see Chapter 8 Who's Who).

This means you can benefit from early reactions to your proposals and improve your chances of a smooth passage through the planning and faculty processes. It is common for the local authority to rely, to an extent, on advice from Historic England and it is important that HE is appraised of your PCC's plans at an early stage. This is crucial if your building is listed and obviously, the higher the listing, the greater the interest.

Hiring a professional

Making a convincing case to the DAC may involve engaging a professional adviser and this will be encouraged by your DAC secretary. This would normally be your inspecting architect or surveyor who would be capable of producing a clear specification and schedule of works. This is covered in more depth in Chapter 2.

Submitting your faculty application

When submitting your faculty application to the DAC, you will need to include as much information as possible (see Note 4). The DAC secretary will acknowledge receipt and inform your PCC when the DAC will meet to consider your application and notify you of any further information they require.

What happens next? The DAC meeting

The DAC secretary will include your application on the next available DAC agenda and circulate to members any additional information that might aid the forthcoming discussion. This might include your Statements of Needs and Significance (see Chapter 3 and Appendix B) and any reports from site visits.

The secretary will brief DAC members at the meeting on your application, which, all being well, will be able to recommend to the chancellor that a faculty be issued. Alternatively further information or a site visit may be necessary before that can happen. Either way, you will be contacted soon after the meeting to inform you of the DAC's decision.

What happens if our application is successful?

If the DAC recommends that a faculty is issued, the secretary will forward a 'notification of advice' to this effect to the PCC. Either the DAC secretary or the registrar will give instructions about the display of public notices – usually one outside the church and one inside the church. If a third notice is requested, this indicates that the DAC believes the work warrants as much public scrutiny as possible and this copy should be displayed in a central location within the community the church serves. Cases where this may occur include works to the churchyard and those which may alter the appearance or character of a listed church – the removal of pews, for example. The notification of advice is not the final authorisation and you should not start work until the faculty is issued.

The DAC notification of advice may be subject to conditions. The chancellor may either delay issuing the faculty until they are fulfilled or make the faculty dependent upon them. The back of the 'notification of advice' indicates other groups that should be consulted if they haven't been already. You or your architect should send details of the proposals to those groups as soon as possible.

The public notices will include instructions for completion, display and return, which must be followed precisely. There is also a requirement that, after display, you send a copy to the registrar with the application form, or form 3a, (traditionally referred to as the petition for faculty form) unless already completed (see Note 5).

During this period, the registrar will review the papers and contact you if more information is needed. He/she will send the papers to the chancellor or archdeacon depending upon the nature of the work, and they will make the final decision. If this is to authorise a faculty, then, once the registrar has received your form 3a and signed public notice, and no representations against the proposals have been received, the faculty document will be issued and sent to you. The work can now finally begin, subject to any conditions specified.

What happens when not everyone is happy with our plans?

Should the registrar receive objections from members of the public or from interested organisations, he/she will contact the objector to see whether the objection is simply to be drawn to the chancellor's attention, or whether the objector wishes formally to contest the application in a consistory court.

As the judge of the diocesan consistory court, a chancellor authorises the issue of faculties but only convenes a court when an objector formally contests an application. The chancellor or registrar will give directions to all parties as to how a contested matter will be dealt with. Expert witnesses may be called on both sides. Court hearings can be expensive and each side may have to bear their own costs with the losing side potentially paying for the costs of the court.

Early consultation with all interested parties and a willingness to make compromises will, in most cases, avoid the need for the formal legal process of a contested faculty application.

Emergencies

Occasionally you may have to carry out emergency work. A ceiling has collapsed or a tree made dangerous by a storm. Emergency work can be completed without a faculty but you need to contact your archdeacon or DAC secretary first. The chancellor is able to grant an emergency faculty without the need for public notices. You may be asked to complete a faculty application form retrospectively.

Variations

It is not uncommon, especially during major repair projects, for the PCC and its architect to have to react to changing circumstances. The condition of part of the building may be worse than originally thought or fundraising may have exceeded expectations, allowing the PCC to redecorate the chancel as well as the nave, for example. The original specification may have to be altered to reflect the change in circumstances and an amendment to the original faculty sought. This is in the gift of the chancellor and he/she is likely to request the DAC's view on the change. The issue may not have to be taken to the full DAC. Instead a standing committee may be convened to review the changed specification and schedule of work. Once the DAC is content with the proposals the matter is passed to the registrar who, after consulting with the chancellor, will issue a letter advising the PCC that the change is acceptable and the original faculty altered to reflect the change.

Temporary re-ordering

A PCC may sometimes wish to experiment with how liturgy is conducted in the church. Your archdeacon is able to issue an archdeacon's licence for a period not exceeding 15 months. More information about archdeacon's licences is included in Chapter 3.

Note 1. The scope of the exemption:

This includes buildings and structures affixed to or within the curtilage of a church so long as the main purpose of these structures is 'ecclesiastical'[9]. Examples of these structures may include lychgates, walls and churchyard monuments. When work is proposed to these structures, the PCC would be wise to discuss the matter with their archdeacon or DAC secretary.

In addition to listed building consent, churches are also exempt from conservation area consent and a building used for ecclesiastical purposes cannot be scheduled as a monument.

Note 2. Changes to come:

During 2015 two lists will be submitted to the General Synod of the Church of England for approval. They will detail work that can be undertaken without the need of a faculty. List A will include minor items that a PCC can do without recourse to anyone, List B will require the archdeacon's approval.

---

9. The Operation of the Ecclesiastical Exemption and related planning matters for places of worship in England – DCMS 2010.

Note 3. The perfect site visit:

. . . is difficult to achieve. However, the key to success is the involvement of as many interested parties with a relevant role in the process. The DAC secretary will normally co-ordinate the visit and will use their contacts with the various organisations to arrange for the right people to be present. Some amenity societies have one national officer and juggling diaries to get everyone on site at the same time may mean the meeting has to be arranged a number of weeks in advance. Ideally, the archdeacon will attend and chair the meeting with the DAC secretary taking notes. Ample time should be allowed for the meeting but a number of visits may be taking place the same day so the DAC and others may have to move on elsewhere. It is important, therefore, to appraise the DAC secretary of all the subjects to be discussed at the site visit before the meeting starts. It is not unusual for PCC representatives to say at the close of a site meeting 'While you are here . . .' This can be frustrating for all if the visiting party needs to move on to another venue.

The archdeacon is likely to start the meeting by introducing everyone and all parties will be given the opportunity to speak. It is vital that all the visitors are able to question the PCC on its plans. Please remember that while the PCC may have been discussing this project for many months, this may be the first opportunity for others to see the plans and talk about the proposals. Questions that the PCC have long ago addressed may be asked again, so be patient. At the end of the visit the chair should sum up what has been discussed and set out the next steps. A written report will be submitted to the PCC normally after the main DAC has had the opportunity to receive it. Other organisations' representatives will submit their views in due course.

Note 4. What to include in the faculty application:

The Standard Information Form (form 1) unless previously submitted;

A resolution from the PCC agreeing the work or proposals;

A specification and schedule of works from the PCC's architect or surveyor;

Drawings to accompany the specification;

Photographs of the areas of the building affected;

If applicable:

Correspondence from interested parties (Historic England, Church Buildings Council, national amenity societies);

Statements of Needs and Significance (if required);

Correspondence with Natural England if bats are present in the church.

Note 5. Regional interpretation:

While there is one set of Faculty Jurisdiction Rules, some DACs and registrars have interpreted them in differing ways. One example is the sending of the form 3 to the DAC with the initial paperwork rather than to the registrar later in the process. The introduction of a national on-line application system will steer PCCs in the right direction indicating the required forms and papers at each stage of the process.

Chapter 2

Repairs

Before your thoughts turn to the Forth Bridge and other visions of a job never done, let's stop and take stock. Many churches, though centuries old, are constructed with the best materials that could be sourced, made and delivered in medieval England. With regular maintenance and the occasional repair, they are likely to continue to remain standing for several more generations to come. But, whether you have an interest in a church with Saxon origins or one built after the devastation of the Second World War, don't panic because there's an abundance of help available to you.

Repairs may appear daunting when most members of a Parochial Church Council (PCC) have little or no experience of maintaining non-domestic properties, let alone the necessary materials that bear little resemblance to anything found on the shelves of a builders' merchants or DIY store.

Your help will come from a variety of sources and you can avoid many pitfalls if this is sought at an early stage. A good place to start is the Quinquennial Inspection Report (QIR) (see Note 1) as this will identify your church's defects and gives advice on what needs to be done over the next five-year period. Your architect/surveyor, the DAC secretary or archdeacon can then advise you on how to proceed.

The Quinquennial Inspection Report (QIR)

Most Anglican places of worship are inspected every five years by an architect or building surveyor who follows up the inspection with a detailed written report. (While both professions are acceptable, for the sake of brevity the term architect will be used). The QIR, which is required by law,[10] is your guide to the construction of the building and details any faults discovered during the inspection. The report concludes with a summary, listing the works in order of priority. Items categorised A must be carried out immediately, B within the next 12 months, C within the next 18 to 24 months, D within the next five years, E represents a desirable improvement but places no timescale upon completion, and M is deemed routine maintenance.

Only architects who are known to have expertise in church buildings and their construction are allowed to undertake these inspections and your local DAC holds a list of professionals known in the diocese who are entrusted to do this work. Do check with the diocesan office how the inspections are arranged and paid for as some diocesan boards of finance pay architects direct and others pass the responsibility of payment to the PCC. The fees vary from diocese to diocese so, if your PCC is responsible for paying, make sure you know how much the bill should be.

There should be a copy of the last inspection report in the PCC's files but contact your DAC secretary or archdeacon if in doubt as to when your last inspection was carried out. Inspection reports can be in paper format but increasingly they are emailed to the recipients. Past copies are a valuable source of historic information and therefore should not be thrown away but offered to the local diocesan records office.

---

10. The Inspection of Churches Measure 1955.

Doing the QIR

The architect will arrange with you a mutually convenient time for the visit. This may take a whole day, depending on the size of the building. The architect will be delighted if all keys and an appropriate ladder are made available and, if your tower has them, the bells hung down so that as many areas as possible of the building are accessible. Ask your architect if he/she would be willing to attend a PCC meeting to present the report and answer questions so that the whole PCC is aware of the issues facing the building in the next few years.

Your QIR report will set out any defects but will not detail how any repairs should be carried out so it won't be possible to use the report to obtain quotes from builders or to apply for a faculty. The QIR is no substitute for an architect's specification and schedule of works which specify materials and the method of repair.

Architects and Surveyors

You are encouraged to develop a doctor/patient relationship with your architect. Over a period of time, the architect will get to know the building well and be a potential source of help and advice. They will be able to track changes in the building from one inspection to another – is that green patch on the wall getting larger or shrinking? The more you get to know an architect the more likely they will be able to give you advice, often free of charge, over the telephone or by email. However, they are professionals and can and should charge. Always check to avoid unpleasant surprises.

Developing this close relationship takes time and the best advice is to avoid frequent changes of architects if possible.

Yet sometimes the personal dynamics feel wrong and a change can be beneficial for all concerned. Ask the DAC secretary for the list of approved architects and speak to other churchwardens in your own or neighbouring benefice in order to find a professional with whom you may be able to work. Make sure any change is discussed at a PCC meeting, a resolution passed and any outstanding invoices settled. This makes it clear that it is a PCC decision and not down to one individual.

While it may be tempting to employ the retired architect, surveyor or engineer in the congregation, it would be prudent to ask: 'Did you work on historic buildings when you practised and are you currently accredited to work in building conservation?' More importantly: 'Did you retain your professional indemnity insurance?' It is wise to assume that not all projects will go well and you need to consider how the PCC would feel about suing a member of the congregation should that unfortunate situation ever arise.

Most, if not all, architects on the DAC list will be accredited as either an Architect Accredited in Building Conservation (AABC) or the surveyor's equivalent – a member of the Royal Institute of Chartered Surveyors Building Conservation Accreditation Register. This accreditation is crucial if you are planning major works that need a Heritage Lottery Fund Grant for Places of Worship (GPOW) (see Note 2). If HLF grant-aided work is to attract fees of more than £10,000 the PCC is required to competitively tender for the architect. This can be a cause of anxiety as an inspecting architect working on a church for some time may not be the cheapest. However, the HLF realises that cost is not necessarily the overriding factor and will be prepared to accept a higher-priced architect if there are good reasons – such as long-term knowledge of the building.

For the want of a nail . . .

Tackling repairs sooner rather than later makes obvious sense. Faults can worsen if not dealt with quickly and material and labour costs can rise over time. There is a lot of truth in the old adage 'for the want of a nail the roof was lost' (see Note 3). A slipped tile creating a hole in the roof will not only allow water to enter the building but may also act as a welcome to bats looking for a cosy new home. Once bats have started to use this hole it will be difficult to repair the roof without affecting them. Since bats are a protected species, all work that may affect bats or their roosts must be carried out with authorisation from Natural England. Deliberate damage to a bat or roost is a criminal offence and can land a PCC, architect or contractor in a great deal of trouble (see Note 4).

Many straightforward jobs can be done without the need for a faculty. Such work will be detailed on a list readily available from the DAC's webpages. Speak to your archdeacon or DAC secretary if in doubt. 'Engagement' is a current buzzword but it really is the secret of success in looking after church buildings. You should feel able to engage with the DAC and vice versa since we all are working with the same aims and purposes. There's no such thing as a silly question so just ask – everyone will be pleased to help you.

While it is perfectly acceptable to use local builders to repair churches, it is vital that you use someone who has sympathy with and understands the building and its materials. I would be very wealthy indeed if I had a pound for every time I heard the cry: 'We would do nothing to damage our church!' I could insert the word 'deliberately' as some of our predecessors have inadvertently caused damage to church buildings simply by embracing new materials too eagerly. The use of cement in render and pointing, or emulsion paint instead of limewash on the internal walls, for example, have led to major problems.

Church buildings need to breathe, and unless yours is relatively new, there is unlikely to be a damp-proof course under the floor and walls, as you might expect to find in your own home. The ever-present natural moisture in the ground and air round us needs to circulate and if the floor is impervious it will use columns and walls like a wick. If the walls are covered in traditional materials such as limewash on the internal surface and lime render externally, moisture will harmlessly pass through and evaporate. Hard cement render or oil-based emulsion paint traps the moisture in the wall and manifests itself as damp patches, flaking paint or blown plaster. You will need expert advice if you are faced with damage caused by the use of inappropriate materials. Please speak to your architect as remedies are often available. They may come at a cost but will certainly safeguard the building in the long run.

The key is to employ an architect knowledgeable in the use of traditional materials. That way, the above problems may be avoided.

Major repairs

So, you have identified a major repair, perhaps from the quinquennial inspection, and you have heard from the archdeacon or DAC secretary that you need to use an architect (see Note 5). The next step is to arrange a visit from your chosen professional. He/she may be familiar with the area that needs to be repaired having brought it to your attention in the quinquennial report, or may be viewing the problem for the first time. When arranging the visit ask whether a ladder may be needed. Don't be surprised if your architect tells you the repair is not worth tackling at this stage. For example, cracking can appear in a church since, with limited foundations compared to modern buildings, it moves slightly as climate change presents us with increasingly wet winters and very dry summers. Such cracks should be monitored but can close up again when weather conditions change.

If the architect recommends repair and the PCC agrees, he/she should be asked to write a specification and schedule of works. This sounds like two documents but is often bound into one. The specification describes in detail the materials to be used: for example, the type of tile to be used, the code (thickness) of lead, the mix of mortar and limewash, etc. The schedule of works describes how the work will be carried out using the materials mentioned in the specification. The contractors will use this document to price the work so the more detailed it is, the easier it is to price and the more accurate the tender will be. The DAC will want to see the specification and schedule of works too, as the committee will base its advice on the soundness of these documents.

In addition to the specification and schedule of works, the architect may produce drawings or marked-up photographs which identify the area of work. These can be very helpful to the builder in identifying the amount of work that needs to be done. 'Rake out defective pointing on the north wall' may be too vague a statement as the builder's opinion on what is defective may vary from that of the specifying architect. A drawing or photo of the wall identifying the defective pointing avoids confusion, allowing a more accurate price to be obtained. This is in your best interest as the PCC will not want vague descriptions in the specification that may lead to the builder carrying out more work than originally intended.

Cost

Once the specification has been written, the architect should be able to give you an indication of the likely cost of the work.

Major repairs need specifications
and schedules of work.

This is a preliminary figure and won't be as accurate as going out to competitive tender – which is seeking a price based on the specification from a number of contractors. At the same time, the PCC can use the specification as the basis for applying for a faculty (see Chapter 1). It is always best to wait until the DAC has made its recommendation before going out to tender in case the DAC suggests changes to the specification that may result in a change in cost.

Once the DAC has recommended the work for approval and the chancellor has granted a faculty, the work can go out to tender. The PCC may be asked if there is a contractor it would like added to those being asked to tender. Don't worry if you don't have one as the architect will know of firms he/she has used for similar jobs in the past. After a set period, the tenders will be returned to the architect and opened at the same time to retain confidentiality. The architect will then write to the PCC informing it of the results. The prices may vary significantly – this is quite normal – and, unless there are very good reasons, the cheapest tenderer is usually asked to do the job.

Minor repairs

These may be small enough to be carried out without your archdeacon's or the chancellor's approval – contact your DAC secretary for advice. However, the PCC may wish to seek three quotes to ensure that they are paying a fair price.

Changes during the contract and emergency work

Even the best-planned projects can hit unforeseen circumstances. Perhaps the work required is more extensive than first thought, perhaps burials have been discovered where previously they were thought not to exist, or maybe the type of material needs to be changed. Since any faculty granted was on the basis of the architect's specification and schedule of work, the faculty needs to be amended to take such changes into account. Check with the diocesan registrar that he/she is happy for the existing faculty to be changed, then contact the DAC secretary with the revised information. The DAC may need to be consulted so inform the DAC secretary if a delay will cause problems on site.

The chancellor can issue emergency faculties often without the need for a completed faculty form or the displaying of public notices. If the work is a genuine emergency then contact your archdeacon, DAC secretary or registrar.

Completion

Once the work has been completed you should send the registrar a certificate of completion signed by the contractor or architect to say that the work, as described in the specification and schedule of works, is complete. On large-scale works there may be what's known as a 'snagging period' when the contractor has to come back to repair any minor faults or snags. Usually a proportion of the contract sum is retained until all the snags have been dealt with and the architect is satisfied the work has been properly carried out. He/she will then issue a certificate to the PCC asking that the retention sum is paid.

Time to celebrate

The end of the repair project should be celebrated as it will have consumed a great deal of time for you and the PCC as a whole. Hold a service of celebration and invite those trusts that may have given you a grant towards the work. They will appreciate being asked even if they are unable to attend. Invite the architect and builders too as they will have become familiar with with the building and formed a relationship with the PCC.

Record the work

All work on a church building should be written up in the church's logbook, together with a copy of the faculty and any guarantee offered on the work. It is advisable to retain all correspondence in a file for reference should something go wrong later.

Note 1.

The national Church Buildings Council (CBC) has introduced a standard format for quinquennial inspections which it hopes architects and surveyors will follow. As well as containing photographs of the areas of concern, the QI report should also provide an estimated budget for the work. Some dioceses insist that reports are in this format. Ask your DAC secretary what format is used in your diocese.

Note 2.

Grants for Places of Worship (GPOW) is the main church repair grant programme funded by the Heritage Lottery Fund. It is aimed at urgent repair work to listed churches and, in addition, offers grants to encourage the wider community to become engaged with the church building. Churches on English Heritage's/Historic England's 'Buildings at Risk Register' are favoured but not at the exclusion of those not on the Register. For a PCC faced with a major (and urgent) repair and happy to accept Lottery money, GPOW should be the first port of call: www.hlf.org.uk

Note 3.

Routine maintenance is the key to a healthy building. In the UK, rainwater is a significant problem for churches and clear rainwater disposal goods are vital to prevent water ingress leading to a wide range of damage to the fabric and contents of a church. If there's any doubt about the efficiency of a church's gutter and downpipe system then you need to don waterproofs and investigate in the middle of a downpour. This is the only opportunity you will have to see your rainwater goods in action. Regular routine maintenance will allow for the clearing of these vital components. Increasingly, dioceses offer a church maintenance scheme – check if yours does. If not, arrange for a local contractor to undertake the work once all the leaves have fallen from neighbouring trees. See if other churches in the benefice or deanery are interested, as it may be cheaper to bulk-buy such services. Some churches' rainwater goods may be easily accessible and can be done with volunteer labour but care must be taken and appropriate risk assessments carried out. It is not a job to be tackled up a ladder with a trowel on your own.

Note 4. Bats

The Bat Conservation Trust runs a helpline – 0845 1300 228 – on behalf of Natural England. Every care should be taken not to affect bats, or their roosts and the timing of your repair project may have to reflect this so as to avoid hibernation or maternity periods. Check with your local wildlife trust if you are unsure whether your church is known to have bats as they may keep records. The Church Buildings Council has produced helpful guidance on the subject available from the ChurchCare website.

Note 5. Architects

Architects and surveyors may seem expensive but their fee reflects their professional qualifications, experience and expertise. Best of all they take the stress away from a churchwarden because they will specify what work needs to be done and, as a result, the PCC is unlikely to have any unpleasant surprises. There are plenty of anecdotes from PCCs who have simply found a builder on the internet. Once on site and following a restorative cup of tea, the builder investigates the problem and sets to work. After lunch and with half the chancel tiles off he/she then delivers the bad news – it's much worse than first thought and the price has just doubled. What do you do? The chancel roof is half off and the builder has you over a very large and expensive barrel. An architect would have prevented this from occurring or would have acted as the PCC's agent should problems have arisen.

Chapter 3

Improvements and Re-ordering

Churches are not always about repairs, sometimes we want to explore how to make the building fit in with our needs. So how can we combine the desire for an inspirational worship space with the functionality to meet social needs?

There are two words that you will come across:

'Re-ordering' has come to mean more than rearranging or adapting churches for liturgical changes. In recent years, it has also referred to secular uses, albeit still retaining the building as primarily a place of worship. However, for the purposes of this book and to avoid confusion, we will use the term as it applies to worship and liturgy and call it 'liturgical re-ordering'.

'Improvements' on the other hand are aimed at bringing the building into the twenty-first century in terms of facilities such as WCs, tea/coffee points and meeting spaces. These can benefit worshippers, visitors and those who use the building for social purposes.

Then there are changes that are aimed at beautifying the church such as new works of art, or the introduction of memorials such as plaques, statues, stained glass, or even items that people have gifted to the church. These can be sensitive areas in themselves but for convenience can be grouped under the heading 'Improvements'.

Liturgical re-ordering

Liturgical re-ordering means changing the current 'order' of the church to enhance the way in which worship is conducted.

This may be achieved by rearranging furniture, removing a number of pews (see Note 1) or perhaps the introduction of a nave altar.

Since the conduct of worship continues to evolve, you might consider it prudent to conduct an experiment to see if any proposed re-ordering will suit the worshippers and provide the inspirational sacred space you may be seeking.

Archdeacon's licence for temporary re-ordering

The Faculty Jurisdiction Rules 2013 allow temporary and reversible changes for a period of 15 months without the need for a faculty. This is known as an archdeacon's licence for temporary re-ordering. Reversible is the key word here, because, at the end of the 15-month period, the PCC must either return the arrangement to how it was prior to the experiment or apply for a faculty to make the changes permanent. Obviously the selling of pews on eBay, or the sawing of timber-work during this period need to be resisted!

Speak to your archdeacon about this simple mechanism in order to try new arrangements. It is straightforward and can cover a wide range of works just so long as it's all reversible. The time period can't be extended so you need to make sure towards the end of the licence you and the PCC have agreed what needs to be done.

Re-ordering on a permanent basis is where the benefits of the ecclesiastical exemption (see Chapter 1) shine. The DAC may or may not have a liturgical adviser but it will certainly have clergy members experienced in today's liturgical practices. The committee will assist the PCC in finding a solution fit for their purposes and provide examples in other churches for the PCC to visit. Such changes need to be handled sensitively and time taken to choose the right course for your congregation.

Improvements

The term improvements covers a wide range of work but can be easily (if widely) defined as being distinct from a repair. A roof repair preventing the ingress of water could well be seen as an 'improvement' if you happened to be sitting under the drip, but technically it would be a repair and this is covered in Chapter 3.

I have mentioned the opening paragraph of the Care of Churches and Ecclesiastical Jurisdiction Measure 1991 in Chapter 1 which states that all those involved in working under the Measure must have primary regard to churches being centres of worship and the church's mission. This is true, but where changes to buildings are concerned, the DAC is understandably a bit more cautious. Changes or improvements must be based on an evidence of need (see page 45 and Appendix B).

Managing change

However pressing the need for change, more often than not there will be resistance and this can come from regular worshippers as well as those in the wider community who may not attend church regularly but nonetheless have an affinity with the building for historical reasons.

Churches are often seen as symbols of solidity and permanence in a fast-changing world and changes to a church building may mean upheaval, disruption, and, in some cases, the pain of loss.

Seek early advice

Even though improvement or re-ordering projects might be new to your PCC and congregation, your DAC should be able to supply you with examples of other churches to visit that have already undertaken successful projects, perhaps very similar to yours.

What works well in one church won't necessarily work in another so it's important not to view your visits simply as a catalogue of schemes to choose from, then deciding to go with a project just like the one at Little Marsh St Andrew.

The purpose of a tour of similar schemes is to enable you to see what is possible and to consider whether this would suit your particular church and circumstances. Make sure you fully engage with other churchwardens and find out if there's anything they would do differently in hindsight. Find out who their architects and contractors were, ask about costs and get them to be candid about any problems encountered during the project. Don't forget to ask about grant bodies and do get them to share fundraising ideas.

Request a site visit

Taking your plans to the DAC at the earliest possible stage will enable them to arrange a site visit to discuss your proposed project. You don't want to have to explain to your PCC why a project five years in the making won't actually work, let alone receive permission.

While it is always very helpful for one person to take the lead within the PCC, they should ideally have a small group round them to share the responsibility. A scheme can quickly become a pet project for an individual – a situation to avoid, especially when hitting a sticky patch. You'll need to be pastorally sensitive about this as people can be very hurt if 'their' project fails to gain favour with the PCC or DAC.

Who else gets involved?

While the Church enjoys ecclesiastical exemption, it does not operate in isolation and this is especially true when it comes to improvements. The DAC will understand this and will probably suggest that it brings other partners to a site visit. These may include Historic England (the new name for the part of English Heritage that provides advice on planning issues), the national Church Buildings Council and the appropriate amenity societies such as the Victorian Society or the Society for the Protection of Ancient Buildings. As we've already learned, it is essential for these bodies to hear the PCC's plans at an early stage – especially in the context of the building – and for the PCC to hear any concerns before ideas become too focused on one particular outcome (see Note 2).

Share your plans

Engagement is another 'must' when dealing with sensitive changes. You'll be wise to engage with the whole community, whether or not they worship in the building, as they are just as entitled to raise objections as a member of the PCC. This can be simply achieved by having drawings on display in the church and writing an article in the local community newsletter.

I don't think it is possible to 'over consult' but you might prefer to regard consultation as 'sharing' your plans. Remember, you don't necessarily have to adapt your plans to embrace every point of view raised.

Statements of Needs and Significance

Two documents will be mentioned throughout the discussions surrounding your plans – the Statement of Needs and the

Statement of Significance. These need to be written for any project where a listed church is to be altered in such a way that may affect the character of the building.

It is a moot point as to when these are produced – starting with a site visit will help you to produce your Statements. Otherwise, a great deal of time and effort may have gone into drafting the Statements when the proposal they are addressing is unlikely to receive support. If the PCC is able to jot down some of its ideas prior to the visit, then those attending will have the benefit of at least some understanding of the PCC's need before the visit takes place.

The Statement of Significance

The Statement of Significance follows a set pro-forma (Appendix B) but will explain the historic and architectural significance of the church in general and, more specifically, the area affected by the proposed work. The purpose behind this is to demonstrate that the PCC is aware of the implications of the proposals. If, for example, pews are to be removed and disposed of, the PCC will already be aware of their age so that the decision to proceed with the application will be made in full knowledge of the facts.

The Statement of Needs

The Statement of Needs also follows a pro-forma but will include an explanation of how the mission and ministry of the church is currently being hampered and how the proposed changes will alleviate this. While your aspirations need to be included, evidence-based information should form the core of the Statement of Needs. It is no use saying that: 'If all the nave pews were removed the PCC is sure all the village groups will want to use the church.' You need to be able to demonstrate that the PCC has received actual enquiries from groups wanting to use the building. Including photographs showing how the pews get in the way of what happens now will strengthen your case.

Those reading your Statement won't be able to come on a Sunday to see how you worship, or attend a group which meets in the church but these activities can be photographed or videoed (most smart phones now include the ability to take short videos) and sent to the DAC to aid the application. Always ensure permission is sought, especially when taking images of children. The Statement of Needs is your opportunity to showcase the public benefit that will result from the changes and, importantly, how this benefit outweighs the historical significance of the object that may need to be removed.

Conservation Management Plans

In certain circumstances, for example when the building affected is a major parish church (such as a building comparable in size to a cathedral,) or the plans are unusually complex or controversial, the normal Statements of Needs and Significance may not be sufficient. Conservation Management Plans (CMPs) are designed to assist PCCs of major churches to manage their buildings on a day-to-day basis and provide information helpful to assisting grant- and decision-making bodies in evaluating applications for funds or advice. More information, including examples of CMPs, can be found on the ChurchCare website www.churchcare.co.uk.

Patience is a virtue

Dealing with such highly significant and important buildings is necessarily complex and time-consuming, so try to be tolerant

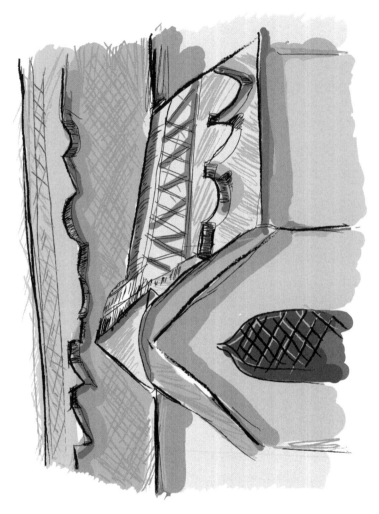

Changes of roofing materials are subject to planning rules.

and patient. Even though the PCC may have been discussing the proposals for years, a site visit may be the first time the DAC and others have seen them. They may need answers to questions which, for you and the PCC, are blindingly obvious. Remember, the visiting party needs to be crystal clear about what you are proposing in order to make an informed decision.

Planning permission

While the Church of England and other major denominations may be exempt from listed building consent, PCCs will need to apply for planning permission if their proposals warrant it. What does this mean exactly?

Fundamentally, any change to the exterior appearance of a church will require planning permission. This would include a change of roofing material or the building of an extension. Permission may even be needed for new noticeboards over a certain size. Do check with your local authority if in doubt.

If you do learn that planning permission is needed for a project, I would advise applying for a faculty first because the level of detail required for a faculty application is often greater than that needed for planning permission. Should a PCC obtain planning permission ahead of a faculty application, they run the risk of the DAC requiring a change to the specification which may mean an amendment to the planning permission.

The DAC will invite the local authority to a site visit if it is thought planning permission may be needed, so that early views can be sought.

Non-monetary gifts

Gifts are sometimes welcome and can be a good way of commemorating the life of a servant of the church if bought in their memory. Such gifts may range from a new chalice to a stained glass window. Whatever the proposed gift, discussion with the donor is vital to ensure both parties are content. A gift may include reference to the person being commemorated. Ideally this should be incorporated into the gift itself rather than on a separate plaque attached to a wall. For example, an inscription can be very successfully be incorporated into the design of a stained glass window or discreetly incorporated onto an item of furniture (see Note 3).

Getting personal

Things get more complicated with proposed gifts of a more unconventional nature, such as: 'Aunt Flo has recently died and we thought you would like her old chintz sofa for the church.' Such well-meaning gifts can be a pastoral nightmare as Aunt Flo's niece may be very upset if the sofa is refused. On the other hand what will the archdeacon say when he/she next visits? Any new items of furniture currently require a faculty and this is your passport to avoiding pastoral meltdown. For example, if the PCC doesn't want to accept the gift of an old sofa from Aunt Flo's niece, explain gently and politely that such an item requires permission to be placed in the church and inform the DAC secretary of your position. It is far more preferable for the faceless DAC to explain that the sofa is unsuitable for the church.

New art

Occasionally, a PCC congregation or donor may propose a new piece of art for the church. Churches have long been patrons of the arts and are increasingly looking to incorporate depictions of community life into artistic pieces such as new windows, sculpture, or textiles.

A stained glass window can commemorate
a servant of the church.

It is worth remembering that, before the iconoclasts went on the rampage during the sixteenth and seventeenth centuries, churches contained many examples of religious art.

Your DAC is likely to have an art and/or stained glass adviser who can guide you through the various steps from concept to unveiling. The Church Buildings Council has produced a guide, *Commissioning new art for churches: a guide for parishes and artists*, available from the ChurchCare website www.churchcare.co.uk. Contact your DAC early on in the process as momentum can quickly build and you want to ensure the approval-giving bodies are sympathetic to your proposals.

Memorial plaques

Memorial plaques, for obvious reasons, are a sensitive area. Families may feel a loved one should be commemorated by the placing of a brass or stone plaque somewhere in the church.

In every case, discussions with the bereaved family will take time and need to be handled with the utmost care and sensitivity. Churches have finite wall space and if every application for a brass plaque or marble monument was to be approved, the walls would quickly fill up, thus excluding future generations.

Chancellors tend to set a very high bar for memorial plaques, insisting that a person to be commemorated should have been exceptional in their service to the Church or that an event should have been of exceptional significance. Try telling a family that their loved one was not exceptional enough to be allowed a plaque and you can begin to see how difficult this area can be.

Raising expectations

The first principle is not to make promises or raise expectations. Instead, make it clear to the family that the matter is out of your hands. Most Chancellors and DACs will have produced guidance you can share with families but it is always best to speak to your archdeacon or DAC secretary at a very early stage. Chancellors may be open to an informal approach but they will at least need a brief biography of the person that demonstrates some of their achievements.

While a recently deceased churchwarden may be fresh in people's memories, try to imagine what a casual visitor might read when memories fade. How will the wording of the plaque tell the casual visitor something about the person's accomplishments? Similar advice would apply to the commemoration of an event.

You will need to be firm at the outset over requests for a plaque – even a small one on the favourite pew of the deceased. Once a precedent has been set it is very difficult to refuse the next request.

New lighting and heating

Perhaps one of the most obvious improvements to a church is the provision of adequate heat and light. Such is the importance of this category that they have a chapter to themselves (see Chapter 4).

Toilets and kitchens

Toilets and kitchens, once regarded as something of a luxury in churches, are now seen to be as a basic necessity for both congregations and visitors. That said, many churches continue to direct visitors to a nearby residence or pub, when they attend baptisms, weddings or funerals, or may even be forced to wave them into the undergrowth in more remote locations.

For PCCs, the installation of a loo is a one-off, whereas your DAC will have overseen all types of installations in scores of, often challenging, locations.

The key, as with so many other projects in important public buildings such as churches, is to start with your DAC secretary who will organise an early site visit. He / she will consider the options with you and put you on the right road to obtaining the necessary faculty.

Kitchens

Before your PCC decides where a kitchen or servery might be accommodated within the church, there are a number of issues to be addressed at the outset.

- Do you simply need a server for hot drinks and biscuits after services?
- Do you aspire to providing harvest suppers or pre-concert canapés?
- Will you need to prepare hot food for a regular lunch club?

That's three possible options and you will need to address those issues in order to explain the purpose of your kitchen or servery in the PCC's Statement of Needs. If your needs rarely extend beyond post-service refreshments, then a simple 'kitchen in a box' may be all you need. These hide the kitchen – normally a sink and drainer with an instant hot water boiler and cupboards – within a piece of joinery. When the kitchen is not in use, all that is visible is a neat piece of furniture resembling an altar-frontal chest or tall cupboard.

Keep it discreet so that it doesn't jar with the overall ambience of your church as a place of worship. If your needs extend to a full-scale kitchen, then you will need to consider screening the facilities from sight, or even an extension. Your DAC and architect will be able to offer guidance.

Do find out what legal requirements and training are needed if you wish to prepare and serve food. The Food Standards Agency's website (www.food.gov.uk) is a good place to start.

Toilets

There are various ways of providing a toilet and your local DAC will be able to give you a list of churches with successful installations. You can then visit those in comparable situations to find the best solution for your own church.

Here are a number of points to consider:

- All new installations have to provide access for all. This means level access and a large enough cubicle for wheelchair users. Your architect will be aware of current legislation.

- If indoor options are limited, you will need to consider a purpose-made building in the churchyard or even an extension to the existing church, though that may be your last resort. Once you have identified your needs, you will need to decide on a location with your DAC.

- We may not have domestic privies at the bottom of the garden any more, but a simple building in the churchyard can provide a toilet and storage and – if it is between the gate and the church – can be convenient for people arriving or departing. I know of one church where their toilet resembles a sexton's hut. It is always unlocked and available to the public as part of that church's service to its community.

- You don't need mains water to have a toilet. Rural churches have installed composting toilets to great effect.

A toilet in the churchyard is worth considering.

There are a number of models on the market and they require only an electricity supply to work. Modern composting toilets are simple to operate. While they have some limitations (they may struggle to deal with 100 people during a concert interval) these toilets can provide the necessary facility at little cost.

While portable toilets might be permitted on a temporary basis, for example for the duration of a concert season or to cover an event, that period should not be extended. Always speak to your archdeacon or DAC secretary about hiring a portable loo for a short period. And certainly don't buy decommissioned ones and hope no one will notice. They may be acceptable at a music festival but they're not a permanent solution for a church.

Toilets and kitchens are often planned together and, with shared services such as water, electricity and drainage, are often located close together. Consider possible pinch points, especially if both are accessed through one door. Try to envisage how people will move around in this area. Will a person conveying hot drinks have to negotiate the queue for the toilet, for example? People tend to linger and chat around service areas. Consider how this may affect access.

Drains and pipes

As we have seen, you can provide a toilet without the need for water or drainage by using a composting toilet. If you have easy access to mains water, you will probably want to connect this to your church to provide a flushing toilet either inside or out in the churchyard. The DAC's archaeologist may be required to have a 'watching brief' when digging a trench for water and drainage pipes in the churchyard. The pipe will need to be buried at a depth that avoids frost damage and it is possible human remains may be found. It is acceptable for these to be reburied, with due dignity, in the trench.

Mains drains should be used where possible but, in rural areas, alternatives need to be considered. If you have sandy soil a 'trench-arch' system of drainage can be used with Environment Agency approval. The EA will conduct a percolation test to make sure that waste water will disperse in the churchyard's soil. A trench-arch system is similar to a French drain and is simple (and therefore relatively cheap) to construct with little impact on the churchyard's archaeology. An internet search for 'trench-arch system' will enable you to watch a YouTube video on how they are made.

The installation of a septic tank in a churchyard can be problematic due to the scale of the excavation required. Human remains are likely to be disturbed if the churchyard has been previously used for burials and, if it is necessary to exhume the remains, the associated archaeology can be costly.

All the above issues reinforce the need to consult with your DAC secretary at an early stage, as you are likely to need at least one visit by the DAC.

And finally . . .

Unlike repairing your church which is usually a straightforward process, re-ordering or 'improving' a building is a more sensitive and complex process and you will need to advance slowly and carefully, weighing up the effect such changes may have on the building against the benefit that will be accrued.

Many church buildings have stood for centuries and, while they may have altered considerably over the years, those changes would have taken place over a period of time rather than overnight.

Always engage with as wide an audience as possible and don't promise anything you can't deliver.

Consult your DAC or equivalent at an early stage and understand help is at hand – often free of charge.

Note 1.

Pews or benches? Technically, pews are enclosed with a door (e.g. box pews), open seats are benches. So generally when we say pew we mean bench but today most church seating – unless a chair or choir stall – is called a pew. For simplicity's sake I will refer to pews and so crave some people's forgiveness.

Note 2.

I once attended a site visit to discuss the location of a WC and kitchen in a town centre church. I thought this might be a difficult meeting as a number of pews were planned to be removed and the amenity society might not be supportive. However, the objections came from some of the PCC representatives who hadn't felt able to express their concerns before. The result, although creating a delay, was further discussion to overcome these fears which should end with a better and more supported solution.

Note 3.

A tip worth bearing in mind for high-value gifts such as a new chalice, is to ask that the name and dedication of the church is incorporated into the inscription. Should a theft take place, the item is much more identifiable and more likely to be returned to you.

Chapter 4

Heating and Lighting

If your place of worship is Victorian or earlier you are likely to face the challenge of providing levels of light and heat to meet the congregation's modern expectations.

This chapter explores some of the heating options and offers some useful points to consider when choosing a new lighting scheme.

Heating

Heating a church will require you to face several, often competing, demands. If the building could speak it would ask for a consistent level of temperature – not too hot and not too cold. The congregation prefers to be warm during a service but might not care what the temperature is when they are not using the building. The parent and toddler group that uses the church on a weekly basis will need warmth but no hot surfaces for small fingers to investigate. The treasurer, with an eye on the fuel bills, will turn the heat down whenever possible (and have the boiler turned off when the church is not used). The green agenda encourages the church to use renewable energy as much as possible.

Increasingly, churches are used for a range of community-based activities outside times of worship. For those with frequent midweek activities one option is to maintain a continuous background heat increasing the temperature for the occasions when the building is used. This will reduce the peaks and troughs of heating and cooling that is so damaging to the building and reduce the sudden surge in temperature from a stone cold church to a reasonably warm one. In turn, the cost of raising the temperature of the building for the comfort of users may be reduced as the building is already maintained at a warm(ish) level. The downside is the fear of significant heating bills as the boiler is always on – and is this green?

Churches used exclusively for Sunday worship may only require heat for a couple of hours a week. A quick burst of warmth followed by cooling comes with the risk of condensation (see Note 1), thus causing problems to the building and its contents. For infrequent use it is far better to heat the people and not the air and the list of alternatives below includes this option.

First, let's look briefly at available fuels, as this will dictate the form of heating available to you.

Fuels and methods of heat generation

Electricity

Widely available although a very few churches remain without a connection. The supply may have to be checked to make sure it has sufficient capacity. Not the greenest energy unless it is obtained from a renewables supplier. Various tariffs are available so check that you are on the best for your use. An off-peak tariff may be suitable for churches only used for Sunday worship. Some churches have installed photo-voltaic cells to produce their own power and this will lessen the cost of energy. Unless the electricity is heating a boiler then most electrical forms of heating warm the person not the building.

Oil

Needs to be stored on site and access available for road tankers. Oil is not a renewable energy source. Tanks need to be bunded to prevent leaks into the environment and can be difficult to locate discreetly, as well as being vulnerable to oil theft.

Natural Gas

More readily available in urban and suburban locations. Like oil, gas is not a renewable fuel but is more efficient.

Liquified Petroleum Gas (LPG)

Has to be stored on site in a secure tank. More expensive than natural gas. System needs to be compliant with Pressure Systems Safety Regulations.

Biomass

Recently of more interest as this is a renewable source of energy. Biomass is a fuel made from wood or other recently living organisms and has low carbon emissions. Biomass is burnt to power a boiler to create heat and therefore needs to be delivered and stored on the site. As the fuel is low density a large storage unit is required otherwise frequent deliveries will be necessary. The boiler needs to be at a high temperature to work efficiently and therefore this may be a viable alternative for a frequently-used church where heating is constantly required to prevent the boiler being repeatedly powered up and cooled down.

Ground source heat pumps

Seen as one of the new wave of technologies transferring latent heat in the ground to your building. The 'mining' of the heat can be achieved in two ways: The first is by running a coil of pipes round much of the churchyard. Water is pumped through the pipes absorbing the heat in the ground. This warmed water enters a condenser increasing the water's temperature further. With this boost, the water is passed into the building's heating system. A significant downside to this method is the amount of excavation in the churchyard and the possible disturbance to human remains this may cause. As a result, the second method – the borehole – may be more acceptable.

The principle remains the same – heat is absorbed by water passing through pipework but the bore works vertically rather than horizontally as in the version described above. There may be some disturbance to human remains as the bore is sunk but, as it is in a small localised area, this may prove more acceptable so long as the necessary precautions[11] are carried out.

Air source heat pumps

In this case heat is drawn from the air outside the church and, via a condenser that boosts the temperature, is used to increase the temperature inside the building. An underfloor heating system may suit this method as the gain in temperature is not significant so works better for a low-level background heat. The cooler the outside air temperature the less efficient the system and so this system may have to be supplemented with another form of heating for the depths of winter.

Water source heat pumps

The same principle as above but extracting heat from water. Bath Abbey is planning a system using heat from the adjacent Roman baths. This example may demonstrate the biggest drawback which is the need for the church to be in close proximity to a water source.

---

11. Such borehole excavation should be avoided in an area with marked graves. Any human remains found should be treated with due care and dignity and reinterred as soon as possible.

Photo-voltaic (PV) panels

These panels have become a familiar addition to many roofs across the country. Generating electricity from the sun seems a wonderful concept and one that has decreased in capital cost over recent years. Yet PV-panels in themselves are not discreet and you may have difficulty gaining permission if your church is listed. However, if your building has a south-facing side aisle with a low-pitched roof then these may be worth considering, especially if the roof has a parapet which can hide the panels from view. A very rough rule of thumb for listed buildings (although negatively expressed) is that if the proposed PV panels cannot be seen by a member of the public standing in a public place, then permission is likely to be granted. Obviously, if they can be seen then rejection is likely. Planning permission is likely to be required as well as a faculty so check with your planning authority early in your deliberations.

Methods of heat delivery

So what type of heat delivery system is appropriate for you? Here is some basic information on options currently available:

Quartz-ray

Description: Heating tubes usually in a horizontal unit attached at a high level to the wall. Electrically powered. Heats people and not the air.

Pros: Cheap to purchase and run. Virtually instant heat-up time.

Cons: Difficult to achieve a discreet fitting as the units are unattractive. Emits light as well as heat and so incompatible with candle-lit services. Heats heads and not feet.

Comments: A reasonably cheap electrically powered solution but the fittings need to be positioned at a high level. This means the walls are often used but some have been attached to moveable poles that (in theory) can be stored when not needed e.g. during the summer. They have been incorporated into suspended light units and a number of designs are coming onto the market. When heating the nave, the units on the north wall are angled to heat the people in the south and vice versa. Checks for wall paintings should be carried out before they are attached to apparently old plaster surfaces.

Under-pew

Description: Electrically-powered convector heaters placed at low level in a pew.

Pros: Discreet. Individually switched so you don't have to heat pews that no one is sitting in. Fairly cheap to run. Increasingly efficient and extra units can be added as funds allow.

Cons: Conservation concerns about attaching to medieval pews due to the expansion and contraction of the timber when the heater is used. Pews really need modesty panels for the heaters to be attached to and prevent draughts. Obviously not workable with chairs. Some don't have grilles to prevent inquisitive fingers investigating the heating element. These can be retro-fitted but seek out those which already have them pre-installed. Cabling and switches can be visually intrusive.

Comments: An ideal solution with the right pews. The heaters are most efficient attached to the underside of the pew thus warming the seat, but they can be placed in front of the person's legs so that they waft heat towards the worshipper.

Seat heaters

Description: These can be likened to electric blankets along the length of pews on which the congregation sit. Electrically powered.

Pros: Individual pew heaters so the whole building is not required to be heated. Relatively cheap to purchase and run.

Cons: Low powered. May provide some heat to lower parts of the body when sitting but won't mitigate against draughts.

Comments: Popular on the Continent. Available in a variety of colours and lengths.

Perimeter

Description: Heaters installed along the walls of the church. They can be small low-level convector heaters, large fan-assisted convector or storage heaters, or gas-fuelled convector heaters boosted by fans. Alternatively, fan-assisted convector heaters can be placed flush with the surface as part of installing a new, or re-laying an old, floor.

Pros: Ideal if there are no pews to attach heaters to. Available in different shapes and sizes and fuels. Can provide quick heat with use of fan assistance.

Ideal if the church is used for a variety of purposes with moveable seating.

Cons: The heaters can be large and therefore not really discreet. Fan bearings on fan-assisted heaters can wear and become increasingly noisy. Flues on gas-powered heaters need to penetrate walls. Prevents the storage of items against the walls.

Comments: Gas-powered heaters require individual external flues for each unit. The flues can be controversial with DACs and are likely to require planning permission. Slimline electric skirting heaters are similar to under-pew heaters and may be suitable for smaller spaces such as chancels or sanctuaries.

Portable gas heaters

Description: These vary from domestic-sized Calor gas heaters to patio-heater-type elements on a wheeled stand with a large bottle of gas attached.

Pros: Instant heat in a reasonably portable appliance. Have the potential to be put away during summer months.

Cons: Produces a significant amount of moisture during the combustion process (approximately five litres of water for every one kilogram of gas). Condensation is the usual by-product of all this moisture which can be harmful to the building and its fittings.

Comments: The portable and heat-producing nature of these appliances is the main attraction but the condensation they produce means they can never be recommended.

Under-floor

Description: Heat rises from electrical elements or water-filled pipework below floor level to give a background heat throughout the building.

Pros: Invisible. Offers heat throughout the building although the scheme can be zoned so that only the space occupied is heated. Kind to the building if left on continually (no wide fluctuations in temperature) so ideal if the church is used throughout the week.

Cons: Expensive to install. Can be archaeologically intrusive. Ideally should be on continually for maximum effectiveness. Leaks may be difficult to detect in a water-based system. May need supplementing if heat output is low.

Comments: There are two ways of generating heat below a floor. The first is a system comprising a series of tubes through which hot water passes. The second version is a system where an electrical current warms heating elements. Both systems may require some excavation of floors to provide the necessary depth for the cabling/water pipes and the necessary insulation below the installation. Care must be taken on the choice of floor covering to allow the heat to rise.

Wet system

Description: This heading covers a multitude of installations but traditionally describes a boiler which heats hot water pumped round a system of pipes and radiators. Much loved by our Victorian predecessors, a system, old or modern, can be effective if regularly maintained – especially if kept free of leaks and furring and equipped with a modern boiler. The boiler can be fired by electricity, oil, gas or biomass.

Pros: When working well, the system can deliver good amounts of heat round the building with temperature control at each radiator. Quiet in operation.

Cons: Heats the air and not the people and therefore much of the warm air will collect at roof level. The convection of the system may create cold draughts from above. May need to be switched on long before service starts. Needs regular maintenance. Pipes and radiators can be hot to the touch. The fixed pipes and radiators may hinder flexible use of the building.

Comments: The wet system needs maintaining to produce heat at an economical level. The system heats the building rather than the people. Boilers and pumps may need attention and pipework can leak, reducing efficiency. When working well it's good – when working badly it may be expensive to run with poor output. The fixed nature of the fittings means that using the building for different purposes may be difficult. Occasionally the temptation is to use the pipework from redundant coke-fed gravity systems. These are not ideal for modern pressurised sealed systems and, while retaining radiators may be acceptable, it is best to replace the old pipework.

Lighting

After wading through the complexities of choosing the best heating system for your church, you may think lighting will be relatively easy.

It certainly used to be in the days of candles and paraffin lamps which, in the case of some small rural churches, are still retained mainly for aesthetic or nostalgic reasons. For churches, it remains the first consideration that the congregation should be able to at least follow the order of service and sing the hymns without straining their eyes.

Yet modern lighting schemes offer a world of possibilities – so much so that clever lighting can transform a dull building into a pleasing one and, conversely, bad lighting choices can relegate a stunning building to the mediocre division.

Your PCC will need to think long and hard before choosing a new scheme that will bring out in the best in the building. You might start with some of the following questions:

- How can we show off to best effect the architectural features of the building such as the roof carvings or the ancient wall niches?

- How can we highlight special areas such as the altar, the lectern or the dais?

- Would our worship benefit from the ability to dim lighting to enhance the liturgy?

- Do we need timed or motion-activated lighting for visitors entering the building during the week or using the WC?

If you are embarking on a major scheme, you might consider that hiring a lighting consultant would be money well spent. On the other hand, your needs may be simpler.

First things first

As we have seen, you first need to determine what purpose your lighting will serve. Is it solely for Sunday services and enabling the congregation to read the order of service and see who is doing what at lectern, pulpit and altar? If so, a simple on/off system may be all that is required. If, on the other hand, you want to stage drama or musical concerts, you may need more flexible controls.

Increasingly, specialists are recommending installations that offer a series of settings controlled from a laptop computer or control console with dimmers, colour changes and other devices.

We need an upgrade

For upgrading an existing system or replacing old fittings, an electrician should meet your needs admirably. Do check, however, that he/she is a member of your insurer's recommended trade body. Look out for the following recognised endorsements: NICEIC (National Inspection Council for Electrical Installation Contracting), NAPIT (The National Association of Professional Inspectors and Testers), or ECA (Electrical Contractors' Association).

We need an overhaul and a new look

I would recommend you start with your inspecting architect and your DAC's lighting consultant who should be able to point you in the right direction.

Professional lighting consultants do exist but will charge the PCC for their time and expertise. Such a consultant might explain how our eyes are naturally drawn to light and that well-positioned spotlights can highlight special features of the building such as a cross or sculpture. They might also tell you how lamps should illuminate, without glare, the faces of people reading at the lectern or preaching from the pulpit. You might also learn how floodlights can be used to 'wash' areas of the building, such as the roof space, while also giving sufficient light to read by.

When considering any professional lighting consultant, your first question should be: what schemes have they undertaken in other churches and could they put you in touch? You will then need to visit the relevant church, not only to experience what has been achieved, but also to speak to PCC members on how they actually use what has been installed. Are the controls easy to manage to achieve the effects they want or do they require a degree in advanced electronics to operate them? One church I know opted for a system that's so complex they tend to use it only on its default setting.

What happens next?

As we have seen, it is always best to consult the DAC's lighting adviser before plans become too advanced. If the DAC needs to visit the church, this should be done at the early planning stage rather than have the committee react to a fully worked-up scheme. A good consultant will suggest a trial in situ to demonstrate the capabilities and performance qualities of the proposed scheme. Inviting the DAC along to this will greatly simplify matters in helping them understand the purpose of your proposals.

Bulbs

Bulbs are referred to as lamps by those in the industry and their technology has rapidly changed with the introduction of Light Emitting Diodes (LEDs). These have two significant advantages over traditional bulbs – they last significantly longer (up to 50,000 hours) and they draw much less power. Better quality LED lamps can also be dimmed. However, you get what you pay for and cheap LEDs will not give you the service you may expect. Better quality units will be more expensive but will reward you with a long life and the added bonus of not having to worry about locating the units in a place where it is easy to reach to change the bulb. There are 8760 hours in a year so, depending on how often the lights are used, you may only need to change a bulb every decade or three. Bear in mind though, that the lamps' 'drivers' will need to be changed more frequently and therefore should be accessible.

Track lighting

DACs and chancellors can be wary of track lighting. Why? Because additional units can easily be attached to the track and the concern is that more and more will be added without an overall strategy. The ease of installation may also trouble the insurer who wants to ensure only qualified people install additional electrical light fittings. Ignore the concerns of your insurer and you may invalidate your insurance. If a track lighting system is for you then ensure the colour of the track itself blends into background to reduce its visual impact.

Surface mounted or pendant?

Pendant lamps offer a wide range of fittings from single lights within a glass globe to ornate chandeliers. Uplighters, downlighters, and even quartz-ray heating elements can be incorporated. One downside of pendant lights is the potential difficulty of changing the bulb as this may require a tower scaffold, a cherry picker or a light unit that can be lowered to allow access.

Wall- or surface-mounted lights are often more discreet as they can be installed high on the wall, or against dark roof timbers. Unless long-life bulbs are fitted, or the fittings are low enough to reach from a ladder, wall-mounted units can also present a problem when replacing blown bulbs. Equally, your church may have medieval or Victorian wall decoration, or a roof of medieval timbers. Attaching lamps and wiring to such surfaces may not be recommended so, before beginning on a once-in-a-generation scheme, take early advice from the DAC and your inspecting architect.

Wires and cables

When submitting an application for approval for a new heating, lighting or any scheme involving new electrical installations, do ensure you include a wiring diagram with your papers. This should show the intended routes of new cables and be in the form of an elevation (i.e. looking at a wall face on) and a plan (from the roof looking down). Cable can be expensive and contractors and clients alike may look at reducing costs by wiring in the most direct way from point A to point B. The result can appear messy with surface-mounted cables running across otherwise clear walls. Be sympathetic to the building and its architecture and lose wires within architectural details or behind mouldings.

Many DACs will insist that only MICC or FP200 cable is used as heavy-duty cable is preferable for public buildings. The cable may have to be installed in a conduit to keep it safe from knocks. High impact PVC conduit is often preferred but makes the cabling more visible due to its bulk and should only be used where necessary. All wiring should be inspected and tested every five years in accordance with the Institution of Engineering and Technology (IET) regulations. Portable appliances (anything that needs to be plugged in) have to be checked too but there is no statutory period for this; it really depends on usage and environment. Contact your insurer for up-to-date advice.

External lighting

External lighting falls into two categories: illuminating paths and entrances to aid access and floodlighting the building.

Illuminating paths

There are a variety of ways to light a path: a series of low level bollards equipped with lights, several lamp standards, or – if the path isn't too long – a light at the entrance of the churchyard and one on the porch or over the principal door. All such lighting may be subject to planning permission and, as a result, you will have to discuss your plans with both your DAC and the local authority. Don't assume 'olde worlde' faux gas-lamps will be preferred over something more modern. They may have their place elsewhere but can look twee. Bollard lighting can be more discreet and cast a glow over the path without undue light pollution. Lights on porches or walls can create glare for those walking towards them. Equally, movement-sensitive examples – sometimes referred to as PIR (passive infra-red) can be disconcerting, although there may be a role for them as security lamps. The church's neighbours won't thank you every time a cat or bat sets off the sensor and the path is bathed in light. It is much better to have a switch at both ends of the path so the lights can be turned on and off manually.

Floodlighting

Floodlighting, not be confused with security lighting, (see Note 2) can impart a positive message (see Note 3). Conversely with poorly designed systems it can also annoy people and cast doubt on the Church's green credentials. It is therefore wise to proceed with caution and plenty of local consultation. Speak to people in surrounding houses and decide how much of the building you want to illuminate and for how long. If your church hosts colonies of bats you may have to delay floodlighting in order for bats to fly out of the building and start feeding. Illuminating throughout the night can be excessive and many churches automatically turn off their lights at midnight. Check with your local authority as planning permission may be required.

My advice would be to find a specialist who has floodlit churches elsewhere and is aware of faculty and planning issues. Aim for a gentle wash which will reduce light pollution as well as softening the appearance of the building. A bright, blast of light will result in hard shadows. LED units are also available for external floodlights and you may wish to see these demonstrated to compare with more traditional lamps such as Son (high-pressure sodium) lights, which give a yellow glow, or metal–halide which emit a whiter light.

Note 1.

Condensation ... The air we breathe contains varying amounts of water depending on how warm the air is. The warmer the air, the more water it can contain. Condensation is formed when warm, moist air hits a cold surface. The warm air cools but can't retain the moisture as it cools and therefore deposits it on the cold surface. So warm air meeting a cold window will cause condensation to form on the glass. Condensation running off glass can cause damage.

Note 2.

Security lighting should be installed in conjunction with a specialist otherwise there is a danger that poorly-positioned units will create deep shadows, thus attracting the activities you wish to discourage. Neighbours are best consulted early as the chosen units are likely to be equipped with PIR detectors which turn on the light as movement occurs.

Note 3.

I recall a postcard dropped in at a church near my home. The church is large, in a rural position but close to a busy trunk road. It is floodlit at night. The author confessed he was not a man of faith but the floodlit church on a winter's night meant that he was almost home from his daily commute. But the significance went deeper – he said that the symbol of the floodlit church in the darkness of a rural night meant something more; something about hope in the blackness, about the undying Christian faith there in the world. I cannot imagine he was the only person to see the church in that way but he was sufficiently moved to write a note thanking the PCC for illuminating the church.

Chapter 5

Church Furniture and Fittings

Churches are not museums we are told, yet the Oxford English Dictionary, offers the following definition:

> A building or institution in which objects of historical, scientific, artistic, or cultural interest are preserved and exhibited.

While churches are primarily places of worship, there is no denying that some contain objects that are of historic and cultural importance – often in a national or international context.

Such objects need care and maintenance if they are not to be lost to future generations. The flip side is that they can be irreversibly damaged if this is done incorrectly. Comparable objects in museums are the responsibility of highly-qualified curators with years of training and often warrant being kept in temperature and humidity-controlled environments. The opposite is true for churches which are freely-accessible public buildings, generally unmanned and often with wildly-fluctuating temperature and humidity levels. While professional curators may be present on some PCCs this is the exception rather than the rule. The saving grace is that expertise on how to care for fixtures and fittings will usually be available at diocesan, and certainly at national, level. Free advice, together with funding that can contribute towards reports and conservation, are available to PCCs, and your DAC secretary should be able to steer you in a useful direction.

The term 'furniture and fittings' loosely covers a whole range of items too vast to describe accurately here. If, therefore, you are in any doubt about an object needing attention, the best course of action is to speak to your archdeacon or DAC secretary and email them with a decent photograph of the item in question.

The day-to-day care of your fixtures and fittings is unlikely to require any special permissions The main thing to remember is that modern cleaning products often contain abrasives which can remove protective surfaces or a patina, thus causing more damage than could be incurred by leaving the item alone (see Note 1).

Conservation (see Note 2) on the other hand, is likely to require your archdeacon's authorisation or a faculty so check with your DAC secretary who should be able to point you to a DAC adviser who can recommend a selection of suitable experts to choose from. Otherwise, conservators with appropriate accreditation can be found via the Institute of Conservation's website (www.icon.org.uk).

The following is a typical, but not exhaustive, list of items that may be found in a church, with tips on how they may be regularly cared for and maintained. More information on all the topics listed below can be found on the ChurchCare website (www.churchcare.co.uk).

Memorial brasses

Metal objects, especially monumental brasses, are normally subject to a patina or tarnish produced by oxidation or other chemical processes due to the interaction of the metal with the atmosphere. This change normally has the effect of making the metal surface dull or even brown in colour. Your first instinct may be to polish the item but you should resist this, as the removal of patina will also remove a layer of the metal surface. To avoid corrosion metal objects should not be immersed in water.

Brasses should be kept clean with a duster and preferably with a biannual application of micro-crystalline wax, which helps resist corrosive elements. Old candle wax can be removed with a plastic or wooden implement – not metal – to prevent scratching.

Cover the brass if bats inhabit the church because their urine and faeces are extremely damaging, decaying to form dilute ammonia, which is alkaline and chemically aggressive. It can cause pitting, staining or etching of porous or polished materials. Monumental brasses are particularly badly affected as bat excretia causes corrosion, which is manifested in a disfiguring and spotted appearance to the surface.

Try to prevent people walking over memorial brasses either by routing them round or covering the brasses. Modern shoes can hold tiny amounts of gravel within the soles, acting like sandpaper when walking over a metal surface. Under no circumstances should coconut-matting or rubber, plastic or foam-backed carpets be used to cover brasses or slabs since they all cause serious damage to anything underneath them. Coconut or other coarse matting traps grit and dirt which will abrade the surface of the brass or slab, while backed carpets can produce corrosion by trapping moisture or giving off harmful chemicals as they deteriorate. Better to cover the brass with a felt fabric over which a carpet can be laid. Make contractors aware of floor brasses and ensure that the protection of brasses (especially from scaffold poles) is included in any architect's specification.

Stained and plain glass windows

Church windows can be strikingly beautiful in their richness of colour, or the way they shaft light into the building.

The total effect, however, comes from their intricate construction. Often they are composed of several sections of glass with grooved leading linking them together and containing glazing cement to prevent water ingress. To prevent the window bowing in the wind, or collapsing under its own weight, the glass and lead is attached to metal saddle bars that are fixed into the surrounding stonework. If all this sounds a bit precarious you need to remember that such methods have been employed successfully for many centuries.

Stained glass windows can contain designs made up of pieces of coloured glass or can incorporate glass with 'painted' (see Note 3) details (such as faces). The paint would have been applied to the glass and then fired in a kiln but, following many years' exposure to the elements, may be vulnerable to flaking off the glass surface. This can be caused by a brush or feather duster moving over the surface. If you have stained glass, medieval or modern, my advice is to consider seriously whether indeed the windows need cleaning. If the PCC thinks they do, or you see painted features flaking from your windows, speak to your DAC secretary or your inspecting architect and consider a professional conservator.

Access to many windows prevents cleaning on a DIY basis as you don't want to find yourself on a ladder with a long brush in one hand waving it in the direction of the glass. You won't be able to control the pressure applied to the brush and damage to the window, or yourself, may result.

Unless your church is relatively modern with simple windows then it's best to seek professional advice if you must give your windows a clean, as they can be extremely delicate.

If a stained glass window suffers damage, always keep the fragments as a conservator may well be able to piece them together or use them as a template or match for replacement glass. A wise precaution is to take detailed colour photographs of stained glass windows. These can be invaluable for restoration purposes.

Sadly, some churches get vandalised and you need to protect the windows externally. There are two options: protective window guards or polycarbonate sheeting. The latter can spoil the effect of the glass from the outside by replacing individual elements of glass with a single pane of polycarbonate. This, over time, may yellow and give the windows of the church a blank appearance. Many DACs therefore prefer window guards which should fit within the individual lights of a window (rather than one guard covering the whole window), and be manufactured from galvanised steel powder-coated in black with stainless steel fixings into the mortar joints of the window's stonework. Such protection may need planning permission so check with your local authority before going ahead.

Wooden furniture

Wooden furniture should be dusted with a soft bristled paintbrush or a soft lint-free cloth and a vacuum cleaner. The nozzle of the vacuum cleaner should not touch the surface because it may damage the object but held an inch or two away and ingest the dust agitated by the brush or cloth. Again, modern materials have to be avoided, including aerosol polish of any description and oils or creams containing silicones. If you must use polish, a block of beeswax is recommended.

Remember, painted wooden objects, such as medieval chancel screens can be very fragile and fragments of paint may be dislodged during cleaning, even with a soft paintbrush. If in doubt, leave well alone or seek professional advice from a conservator. Grants may be available for the conservation of historic painted surfaces, including the production of a conservation report. Ask your DAC secretary for information or search online at the Institute of Conservation(www.icon.org.uk).

Insects love old buildings and you need to be alert to damaging activity. Small holes are an obvious sign of beetle attack but those with a small pile of sawdust below indicate active beetle infestation. An accredited conservator will advise you on how to prevent the spread of such activity. Medieval paint can be affected by chemicals used in pest control and so again any treatment is best left to those with expertise in dealing with outbreaks in historic buildings.

Finally, your nose is a superb early warning system. Decay will produce a smell rarely experienced in a modern house. Alert your architect or DAC secretary if you experience an odd aroma, as an expert should inspect the offending article to prevent the spread of any fungal attack.

Books

Many churches contain historic books such as lectern Bibles, prayer books and possibly even a copy of Paraphrases by Erasmus as directed by Edward VI. Parish libraries still exist in some churches and their contents can be susceptible to age-related degradation so need to be cared for appropriately.

Extreme care needs to be taken when opening an old book as the pages and binding may be weak. Opening a book flat on a table is not a good idea since some can't open wider than 90 degrees without damaging the binding. Contrary to what you may have seen on television, it is considered better not to wear gloves when handling books, as your fingers are more sensitive without them. Just ensure you have clean hands and don't snack or drink as you browse, as it is all too easy to drop a crumb or spill a liquid.

Painted wooden objects, such as medieval chancel screens, can be very fragile.

You can protect the binding of old books by storing them upright rather than leaning to one side. Keeping them out of direct sunlight and in a well-ventilated area will help prevent the formation of mould and condensation. Usually only the top edge of the book needs cleaning and this should be done with a soft-bristled brush with the book held firmly shut. Avoid the use of any leather creams as these may stain or make the book sticky, thus attracting dust.

If books have to be packed away, always wrap them in acid-free paper and not plastic which will degrade over time. Contact your DAC secretary for advice on conserving or repairing books or consult www.icon.org.uk for more information and a list of conservators. The conservation and any disposal of old books will require a faculty so please consult your DAC secretary or archdeacon.

Clocks

Many churches retain a tower clock (sometimes referred to as a turret clock), often still wound by hand. Electric auto-winding has been installed onto the clock mechanism in a number of churches in order to alleviate the need for manual winding. Either way, the clock itself, often a thing of mechanical beauty, needs only the occasional clean and this should be done by a professional clock maker experienced in maintaining historic turret clocks. Resist the temptation to lubricate cogs and wheels. The oil attracts dust which, aided by the movement of the mechanism, turns into an abrasive paste and prematurely wears the metal components. A maintenance contract with a clock maker will include an annual visit to inspect the mechanism as well as the weights, hands, and dials.

Clock mechanisms need only the
occasional clean by a professional.

Pipe organs

For many centuries organs were the most complex machine known to man. Their mechanical systems are often contained within an ornate case and represent a splendid mix of science and art. Looked after regularly, the organ can last for generations but unsympathetic alteration can destroy a valuable piece of our musical and ecclesiastical culture. Every DAC will have an organ adviser and if you are considering any work to your organ it will be necessary for you to consult with him or her. Most work will require a faculty except tuning.

Organs are vulnerable to damage from roof leaks and should be immediately protected should damage to the roof occur. Poorly-sited heating units can dry out leatherwork, warp wind chests and cause tuning problems so consideration should be given to the instrument when planning a new heating system. Most organs will benefit from two tunings a year – before Easter and Advent. The organ's motor will cope well with one service every two years but any asbestos contained in the motor's housing will have to be removed by specialist contractors.

Very occasionally, a PCC may consider replacing their pipe organ with a digital electronic instrument. It is vital the PCC consults with the DAC at an early stage as the importance of the existing pipe organ may not be fully appreciated and disposal may not be straightforward. In addition, the Chancellor may require a church disposing of its organ to find another willing to purchase it as a working instrument and is likely to seek the views of the national Church Buildings Council.

The British Institute of Organ Studies (www.bios.org.uk) has introduced a Historic Organ Certificate which grades organs in a similar way to which buildings are listed. More information can be found on the BIOS website.

Bells

Bells and bell frames have been installed in our churches for generations, with the introduction of change ringing in the seventeenth century allowing ringers greater freedom to ring peals for worship and mark special events. However, many bells pre-date this and it is hard to think of another original object that produces the same sound today as it did when first made. As a result, the retuning of old bells is something that can be controversial and advice from the DAC should be sought early on in the PCC's deliberations.

Timber bell frames are likely to be more flexible than those made from steel and, as a result, the 'go' of the bells may be affected. This movement is generally caused by the frame's joints rather than the timber sections and watching the frame while the bells are rung gives a good idea of the extent of the flex. But be careful, – always wear ear defenders and keep well away from moving bells.

You may have to consider repairing your old timber frame or installing a new, steel version if your ringers believe the frame has excessive movement. Bells' bearings don't cope well with flexing frames and the cost of attempting to stiffen a timber frame can be considerable. Again, when considering repairing an old frame or introducing a new frame, involve your DAC's bells adviser and the Church Buildings Council early on in your planning process.

Should a new bell frame be necessary, the original may, depending upon the age and type, have to be retained in the tower. These frames may be centuries old and a testament to the medieval carpenter's craft and skill. Leaving the frame in the tower and positioning a new frame lower down, gives several advantages:

- The sound of the bells close to the church may be reduced in volume and improved in tone;

- The weight of the bells and frame lower in the tower will reduce any movement of the tower structure;
- The cost of removing the old frame is not incurred;
- The old frame can be used for lifting purposes when installing the bells and new frame;
- The frame is retained for historical interest.

Just like buildings, bells and bell frames may be listed as historically important. The Church Buildings Council hosts the database which is available to search online at www.churchcare.co.uk.

Advice may also be obtained from the Central Council of Church Bell Ringers with contacts for advice and publications at www.cccbr.org.uk

Much day-to-day maintenance can be undertaken without the need for a full faculty.

Wall paintings

One of the biggest threats to wall paintings is damp. If a patch of discoloured plaster develops on or near a wall painting this may indicate a leak in the building's gutters or downpipes and needs to be addressed immediately.

Many medieval wall paintings in churches were painted over in the past and remain invisible to us today, yet still survive under layers of limewash. Old plaster can be recognised by a wavy, contoured finish while modern plaster is much more even and smooth. If your church has what appears to be old plaster, it is best to assume wall paintings exist below the surface. On a day-to-day basis their potential presence should not cause you any problems, but resist driving a nail into the wall to hang a banner or picture. Redecoration may include the removal of loose plaster and it would be wise to take this opportunity to have a wall paintings conservator visit the church to undertake a few test scrapings to see if anything will be revealed below the surface.

Previously uncovered paintings may be vulnerable to damage if the paint is not well consolidated to the wall. Such wall paintings should not be dusted, to prevent paint becoming loose and detaching from the wall. Any pieces which may have come loose should be retained as a conservator should be able to reattach them.

Textiles

Strong sunlight is the enemy of textiles and, in churches, altar frontals, hangings and curtains should be protected if at all possible. Cleaning should not go beyond a very careful annual vacuum with the machine on its lowest setting and a net attached to the nozzle with an elastic band. Hand brushes or vacuum cleaner brush attachments should not be used.

Textiles as wall hangings should be inspected to make sure they are secure and there is no evidence of damp between the wall and the hanging.

Altar frontals should be stored in a chest, carefully hung and not tightly packed, and vestments hung on padded hangers in a well-ventilated wardrobe or cupboard. New altar frontals are likely to require a faculty application. Most DACs have a liturgical adviser who should be able to help you when considering new designs.

An accredited conservator should be employed where repairs need to be carried out and your DAC secretary will advise on what permissions are necessary.

Precious textiles will need protection
from strong sunlight.

Monuments

Monuments may be made from a range of materials including metal, stone, alabaster, marble or wood. All fall victim to wide variations in humidity and temperature which means it is vital to ensure that the building is rain and weather tight for their protection. The utmost care should be used when cleaning monuments and a light dusting with a soft brush should be all that is required. Again, modern cleaning materials are the enemy. If you have a monument with flaking paint, steer clear and call in a conservator to advise on a programme of stabilisation.

Flowers should be placed well away from monuments and other historic objects to avoid irreversible damage from spills and misting. Lilies should preferably have their stamens removed to avoid staining vulnerable surfaces.

Note 1.

When I was a young child I took an interest in coins and one day came across a ha'penny that my book suggested was quite rare. Knowing there was a coin shop in town I saw the opportunity to cash in. I borrowed my mother's silver polish and cleaned this piece of metal until it shone more brightly than when it was first minted. I then proudly took it to the shop for a valuation where I was told it was worthless. The hours spent polishing it had eroded much of the coin's surface and although it looked very shiny, it was now very, very worn. This was the beginning of the end of my coin-collecting hobby but a lesson had been learnt. The wrong material in enthusiastic but amateur hands can spell disaster.

Monuments can take the form of ledger slabs.

Note 2.

Conservation not restoration. There's a significant difference between the two and current policy is to conserve what's left rather than restore what has been lost. This may come as a surprise when a PCC has spent a five-figure sum on the conservation of wall paintings and there doesn't appear to be much change. The conservator will have painstakingly ensured that built-up grime has been carefully removed and that any flaking paint has been reattached to the plaster. They will have certainly resisted the temptation to fill in the 'missing bits'.

Note 3.

The science of stained glass window making is a fascinating subject and one I recommend readers investigate further. Not only will further reading help you to care for these precious pieces of art but also to appreciate the medieval manufacturing process. The ingredients for the colours and painted features will have been derived mainly from enamels and metal oxides which will have changed chemical composition during the firing process resulting in bright vivid colours, sombre shades or black lines depending on the metals employed.

Chapter 6

Churchyards

God's Acre, churchyards, or graveyards are all familiar names for the area of land surrounding a church. Their primary function is to commemorate the dead, although such areas are increasingly seen as amenity spaces for the living community and as havens for wildlife.

Burials and cremations

Anyone living in the parish or who has died in the parish has the right to be buried in the churchyard or to have their ashes interred there, unless the churchyard is considered full and has been formally closed through an Order in Council[12] (see Note 1).

Full burials

While cremations are increasing, full burials remain commonplace where space allows. Increasingly, green burials are being requested with no chemical or non-biodegradable substances being involved in the preparation of the body or coffin.

Ideally, each churchyard should have a plan indicating who is where and it is never too late to start this process. Some PCCs allow families to reserve a plot (see below) and an accurate plan will make the location easier to record, thus avoiding difficult situations in the future.

---

12. An Order in Council is the culmination of a process ending with the Queen approving the Order's contents and is the name given to the document which, in this case, legally closes the churchyard.

A single commemoration stone to mark cremated
remains can be a dignified solution.

Unless sifted, surplus soil from the grave may contain dislocated bone fragments so surplus soil always needs to be treated with care. Some diocesan chancellors allow for a small amount to be disposed offsite by the gravedigger after sifting but the disposal of larger amounts will require a faculty. Consult your archdeacon or DAC secretary before acting.

Cremated remains

As mentioned above, burials of ashes are increasing in number and some churches, with the authority of a faculty, set aside an area specifically for this purpose.

You will need to consider the proposed area, how it is to be demarcated and how the burials will be commemorated. Will it be by individual stones, by one central memorial, or by a memorial book in the church? Ask your DAC secretary for the names of other churches that have already done this so you can visit them to see what will work best for you and your community.

When creating an area specifically for cremated remains, a popular option is to mark the plots with individual plaques or tablets positioned over the area of interment. These can act as a personal focus for the grieving family. If the PCC is considering this as policy, think about the size of the plaque and how many you can accommodate in your designated area. Large stones will quickly fill an area and you may soon be forced to apply for an extension.

Consider the maintenance of the area: if the stones stand proud of the surface, how easy will it be to mow the grass in between? Will you allow flower vases which may have to be removed for cutting then replaced? How far apart will the stones have to be to avoid resembling a pavement which might be at odds with a rural setting? One central stone commemorating all buried in the area can be dignified but will not have the personal touch that some prefer.

The faculty for the area can allow plaques to be attached to adjacent walls provided they are in reasonable condition. Names recorded in a memorial book in the church can be used as a basis for prayer but can only work if the church is left unlocked for visitors.

Ashes are commonly interred in a container – ideally biodegradable – but may be poured directly into the ground. The advantage is that more burials can be accommodated, providing the memorials are in the form of a central stone or the names recorded in a book.

Grave reservations

Relatives occasionally wish to reserve a grave space so that they can be buried near a loved one. A PCC must agree, with a recorded minute from the meeting, that it is prepared to allow such reservations. The reservation must be done under faculty with the family dealing directly with the registrar. Normally the applicant must be middle-aged or above and have some close connection with the parish. A fee is usually paid to the PCC as a contribution to churchyard maintenance expenses.

Headstones and memorials maintenance

Erecting a memorial stone

Faculty jurisdiction applies to everything within the area of the churchyard including the provision of headstones. Because it is patently unrealistic for every headstone to require a faculty application, each chancellor has developed a set of rules delegating the approval of headstones, within certain limits, to the parish priest (see Note 2).

Individuals or families who request a stone not covered by the rules will need to apply for a faculty but this would need to be accompanied by a statement of justification, including any special circumstances relating to the deceased. The matter would then be referred to the DAC and, with its recommendation, to the chancellor. To avoid disappointment, you will need to explain to relatives at the outset that success in their application cannot be guaranteed.

With the cost of stone falling due to inexpensive imports from India and the Far East, and a wider range of designs being produced by wholesalers, there is a greater temptation for families to request memorials that fall outside the rules. It is the clergy who are charged with authorising new headstones and it is imperative that such applications are checked thoroughly before they are authorised. Do ensure all questions have been answered fully, leaving nothing in doubt, well before the headstone is erected to avoid unnecessary distress to relatives.

Some families may prefer wooden memorials instead of headstones and you will need to check whether these are allowed within your local regulations.

Great sensitivity should be applied when dealing with grieving families and, as soon as you are faced with an application that seems out of the ordinary, it is best to pass it to the diocesan registrar, archdeacon or DAC secretary. This may help take the heat off those who live in the community.

More information regarding local diocesan rules will be found on diocesan websites and the Churchyards Handbook (See Chapter 9, Further Reading) contains much more detailed information.

Maintenance

The care of headstones and memorials is the responsibility of the family and, if work is required, contact with the family may quickly resolve the issue. However, if the family has moved away from the area, died out, or simply chosen not to reply, the PCC – as the organisation with ultimate responsibility for the churchyard – must deal with the problem.

Different rules apply with a closed churchyard (see below) but if the churchyard remains open, the PCC will need to make the memorial safe.

Modern, lawn-type headstones typically have a foundation just below ground with protruding dowels to secure the stone. Over time, the mortar securing the dowels may deteriorate and the headstone can become loose. The more traditional monolith headstone, with a significant part of its length buried in the ground, is anchored more securely even if it does not remain entirely vertical as time passes.

A simple but hefty shake of a headstone should demonstrate how securely it is fixed. Always lay a dangerous headstone flat until it can be properly re-erected, while being aware that horizontal stones can become trip hazards.

Most repairs or the permanent relocation of a memorial will require a faculty and advice should be sought from the registrar, DAC secretary or archdeacon.

Vaults

Table-top tombs, contrary to popular film and fiction, don't contain bodies but often stand above subterranean vaults. The vaults are generally constructed of brick with a barrel-shaped roof. The apex of the roof is often quite close to the surface and it is possible over time for the roof to weaken and cause a collapse. I have seen tombs partially or totally sunk inside a vault. Another sign of a vault collapsing is a hole suddenly appearing in the churchyard. Vaults can be several metres deep, so rope

Table-top tombs can sink over time
and will need attention.

off any suspect tombs or vaults and contact the archdeacon or DAC secretary and your insurer. The vault can probably be filled in, but this will need a faculty with the diocesan archaeological adviser specifying the material to be used.

Over time, memorials may have been moved from their original location, which means there may be unmarked vaults within the churchyard. Care must therefore be taken when vehicles such as builders' trucks, cherry pickers, or visitors' cars leave access paths. It is best to avoid using a churchyard as an official or unofficial car park. If this is unavoidable, such car parks should be created only under faculty where evidence has been produced by the PCC that no vaults are under the proposed parking area.

Exhumations

As from 1st January 2015, the Burials Act 1857 has been amended so that any removal of human remains from a consecrated churchyard will need only a faculty, and no longer a Ministry of Justice licence as well. Do speak to the diocesan registrar at the earliest opportunity if any exhumation is proposed.

Extensions to churchyards

In some circumstances, it is possible for a churchyard to be extended to provide additional ground for burials. This will usually require planning permission for change of use and the extended area should be formally consecrated by a bishop. Your diocesan registrar will be able to advise on the process.

Works in churchyards

Poets and novelists have long used rural churchyards to evoke a timeless English scene. It is one that can stir emotions in a local community and any changes in the churchyard landscape need to be carefully planned. If you intend to undertake any work in your churchyard other than routine maintenance or gravedigging, do contact the DAC secretary to see what permissions are necessary. The faculty process with 28-day public notices offers some protection from adverse public opinion after work has been done. The requirement to display public notices will alert people to the PCC's plans before work commences. Being proactive and clearly communicating your plans well in advance through the community magazine or website is far better than having to face a microphone at the local radio station afterwards.

Trees in churchyards

The comments above are equally important in the case of trees. While some works, such as planting, and pruning or felling dead or obviously dangerous specimens may be a matter of applying for permission from your archdeacon, a faculty is likely to be required for all other work. You also need to be aware of trees that are subject to a local authority Tree Preservation Order (TPO). A TPO makes a range of actions a criminal offence, including wilful damage or destruction without the authority's permission.

Working for wildlife

Churchyards are relatively free from herbicides and pesticides, making them a haven for wildlife. PCCs are increasingly recognising this and managing their churchyards accordingly. One way to avoid complaints about the churchyard looking overgrown and untidy, is to mow paths through the grass, which not only allows easy access for tending graves, but

A mown path through a wildlife churchyard
indicates a clear management plan.

shows your wildlife management plan has been carefully worked out. A wildlife interpretation board will reinforce this impression and helps to identify what can be seen in the churchyard.

Your county wildlife trust will probably be glad to offer advice and assistance, including ways in which the local school might benefit by using the church as an educational resource. The charity Caring for God's Acre (www.caringforgodsacre.org.uk) has published a wealth of excellent material.

Churchyards as amenity spaces

It is not only bees and butterflies that can enjoy churchyards. People visit churches for a variety of reasons and a tranquil churchyard can be a pleasant spot for a picnic. A well-placed bench can benefit relatives visiting the graves of loved ones or tourists exploring the area. Always check with your local DAC what permissions are required regarding styles and siting of benches.

Noticeboards

The churchyard is the obvious location for a church noticeboard. The introduction of a new noticeboard will be subject to a faculty and possibly, depending on the size, planning permission. Check with the DAC secretary and local authority. Noticeboards should be positioned so that they can easily be read by all passers-by and I recommend that they include, as a minimum, the current priest's name and phone number (see Note 3). Different dioceses may offer advice on the format for noticeboards and some may encourage PCCs or benefices to adopt a 'house style'. They must be kept up to date and posters advertising past events should be removed as soon as possible.

Closed churchyards

Once a churchyard is formally closed to future burials (a legal process involving the Ministry of Justice), there is no current mechanism for reopening it, although a faculty may allow for the interment of ashes (see the section on cremated remains). Control and responsibility for a closed churchyard remain with the PCC but it may, by formal notice, transfer maintenance to the parish council or other relevant local authority. PCCs may regard the transfer of maintenance duties as a burden lifted but, since there is no clear definition of the standard required and because of budget constraints, it is not always possible to get the local authority to fulfil the PCC's expectations.

The above applies not only to routine grass-cutting and the like, but also to unsafe gravestones where the family cannot be traced, war memorials, churchyard crosses, boundary walls, fences or hedges. There is a residual responsibility for safety on the PCC, and it should still monitor a closed churchyard maintained by a local authority, notifying it promptly of any problems concerning safety. The PCC should also maintain public liability insurance.

The other point to remember is that all Church of England consecrated land is subject to faculty jurisdiction, even if the churchyard is closed (see Note 4) and you may have to remind the local authority of this if it is planning work that requires a faculty. In larger closed churchyards, it may be possible for the local authority to reach an agreement with the DAC and chancellor that, providing all work is carried out within agreed parameters, individual faculties will not be required. Speak to your diocesan registrar if you believe this may apply in your situation.

Note 1.

There are certain exceptions: a churchyard may have closed but those with a reserved space made prior to the closure will still be able to be buried there. Ashes may be buried in a closed churchyard with the authority of the faculty. As you can imagine, most matters relating to churchyards can potentially create pastoral difficulties if not dealt with sensitively. Your registrar will be able to assist you with the current legal situation.

Note 2.

Among pastoral minefields, the matter of headstones is the most dangerous, so much so that I have known clergy to vow they will never move to a church with an open churchyard again.

The Churchyard Rules for each diocese are written with local conditions in mind. You don't have to be an ecclesiastical expert to recognise the cultural importance of a typical English churchyard in the landscape and part of this is the limited range of stones in the churchyard compared with the variety seen in a local authority cemetery. The Churchyard Rules for each diocese will vary due, in part, to regional differences across the UK. It is important to you, your community and your successors that you adhere to those Rules. Memorials falling outside the Rules are not automatically disallowed but will be subject to a faculty application.

Note 3.

I heard of a church with a notice board that said 'Welcome to St Mary's' and nothing else. This is a fine proclamation but it wasn't any good to the person reading it after seeing smoke coming from the nave roof. As well as 999 who else was this person to ring? The vicar or a churchwarden's name and telephone number would have been very useful. When including a phone number, don't forget to add the area code as mobile phones require this and not everyone passing by will know the local code.

Note 4.

In the Church of England, churchyards are consecrated ground (meaning land set aside for sacred use) and may have been used for burials for centuries. The absence of headstones does not necessarily mean a corresponding absence of burials. It was only in the past 200 years that stone memorials became readily affordable. If the churchyard surrounds a medieval church it is far better to assume that burials are everywhere, marked or not.

Chapter 7

Funding

Our churches have none of the state funding that our European neighbours enjoy. We are largely on our own, relying heavily on voluntary donations, although there is some Government help with a VAT refund system known as the Listed Places of Worship Grant Scheme (see page 118).

An array of trusts offer grants and loans for repairing and improving places of worship providing you can meet their conditions. But since December 2012, the key source of funds for listed churches has been the Heritage Lottery Fund (HLF) through its Grants for Places of Worship (GPOW) programme. You can apply for grants from £10,000 up to £250,000 and, providing your PCC or congregation has no objection in principle to accepting lottery funding (see Note 1), the HLF is a useful place to start. Securing a significant grant to start with also improves your chances of attracting other funders.

Remember though, that the priority for the HLF when it comes to GPOW funding is structural repairs 'urgently required within the next two years' that have been clearly identified in a condition survey or your quinquennial inspection report.

Grants for Places of Worship (GPOW)

HLF grants come from public money so, if you are a recipient, you will be expected to demonstrate some benefit to the wider community. The two key outcomes the HLF seeks when making GPOW grants are:

a. that as a result of the grant your 'heritage' – that's your building – will be in better condition

b. that more and a wider range of people will have engaged with heritage

The first is straightforward because you would certainly hope that major repairs would leave the building in better shape than when you started! The second might involve activities such as educational visits, heritage workshops, new guidebooks, or a website about the history of the church. There are endless ways in which you might involve the wider community. Visit HLF's website (www.hlf.org.uk/our-projects) to see some of the projects they have funded if you need some ideas about how to engage more people with your building.

The above two outcomes are absolutely necessary for a successful application but there is an optional extra available with the GPOW grant. It is about making the building itself more user-friendly for the community and for other visitors by providing new capital works such as toilets, kitchens or better heating. The HLF will fund this work up to 15 per cent of the total overall project cost but the work must benefit people beyond the existing congregation.

Before you spend time on the two-stage application process, the HLF suggests you complete a 'project enquiry' form to ensure that your project is on the right track for success. Assuming you get the green light from the project enquiry, you'll need to submit a first-round bid for the 'development phase' outlining your project and stating what help you will need to develop the second phase which is the 'delivery phase'. Do ensure that you include in your application how the project will benefit your local community and make it clear that you have consulted them.

Once you have the money from the development phase, you then use this to prepare your second phase. You need the development money to contribute towards the cost of, say, a builder opening up the roof to see how bad it really is and the cost of an architect to oversee this work. This exploratory stage prepares all concerned for the main contract by accurately (as far as possible) judging the scope of the necessary work.

Why two phases? The logic goes that, during the development phase, your professional adviser will be able to gauge more accurately the extent of the work so that the grant can be calculated from solid research rather than guesswork. This way you can avoid accepting a grant that is not sufficient to meet your true needs. It also means you can ask for some financial support to help with work in your development phase, such as bat surveys, archaeological investigations or other specialist work.

All HLF forms need to be completed online. You can print out a draft if you find it easier but your form must be submitted online. The important thing is not to be daunted by the questions on the application form and give yourself plenty of time to complete it. The guidance accessible from the website is a must-read and it takes you through the process step by step so you can tackle it in bite-sized chunks.

The HLF specifies that you make a contribution towards your project though this can be in cash, volunteer time or non-cash contributions or a combination of the three. They call it 'partnership funding' and some of this must come from your own church's resources. You will also need to prepare a management and maintenance plan and send it in with your second-round application. This is a relatively simple document that clearly sets out how you will look after your building over a ten-year period after the HLF-funded work is completed. Guidance on writing a management and maintenance plan is also available on HLF's website.

Other organisations are also are more likely to help churches and chapels who can demonstrate they are willing and able to fundraise themselves. So rather than sitting back and waiting for the grant cheques to fall on the doormat, you should be planning activities and events to raise money locally. Engaging with the wider community from the start will help you establish a genuine need for your project, evidence of which will be required from your funders as well as the Diocesan Advisory Committee (DAC).

Your diocese may hold a list of grant-making trusts and your local authority library may offer free access for charities to online databases of funders or even an external funding officer from whom you could seek advice.

Fundraising can be fun

Fundraising can pull together the wider community to look after their church but do make it fun. It is not an endurance test! Be open about your needs, not only about the amount to be raised but also the cost of the repair and how much the PCC already has in its bank account. Be aware of the language and symbolism you use – that giant thermometer in the churchyard can be overwhelming when at its lowest point, and a 'Please help' sign smacks of desperation. If you aim to be positive and inclusive – this is your church – you are far more likely to appeal successfully to people's generosity.

Consider fundraising for other good causes at the same time by splitting the proceeds between the church and other charities. This will raise the profile of the fundraising event and will attract greater publicity. You'll need to state the purpose of the fundraising in your publicity but don't be too specific. Making clear it is for St Mary's fabric fund allows you some flexibility but saying it is for repairs to the porch means it has to be spent solely on the porch (see Note 2).

Top 10 tips for completing grant applications:

1. Take time to study the criteria of funding bodies that might help. If you are in Liverpool, don't apply to a trust offering grants to chapels in Newcastle 'just in case'.

2. Never simply send out a standard letter but take the time to make an individual appeal explaining why your church needs the trust's attention. Say what you have already raised and include the difference between what you have raised and the estimated final cost.

3. When completing a form by hand try to keep your answers concise and within the space allowed.

4. Limit how many additional papers you attach to your application while ensuring you attach everything requested.

5. Not all trusts meet frequently so allow sufficient time to apply.

6. Include photographs of the damage or even a film clip with a churchwarden's commentary to add weight to your request for funds (see Note 3).

7. Remember that trusts will target churches which need assistance the most. If you have £100,000 in the bank and are applying for grants towards a £20,000 repair, prepare to be disappointed.

8. Always double check that you've included VAT when applying for funds. Finding out that the costs are 20 per cent higher than you anticipated can come as a nasty shock.

9. Supply details of a contact who is knowledgeable about the work and can answer questions if necessary.

10. Always send a letter of thanks if you are successful and invite the trust to any service of celebration after the work is completed.

Who needs Friends?

Friends organisations can assist churches by getting alongside the PCC for the purpose of fundraising, freeing up others to focus on mission and ministry.

Sound advice on setting up a Friends group has been produced by the Diocese of Canterbury, available from the Parish Resources website (www.parishresources.org.uk), and the National Churches Trust (www.nationalchurchestrust.org.). Friends are not necessarily interested in the mission and ministry of the church but they are keen to safeguard the building from deterioration or closure due to lack of repair and maintenance.

A separate charity

A Friends group can be a charity separate from the PCC, whose main aim is to raise funds for the fabric of the church building.

Having a PCC representative on the Friends management committee will enable a smooth liaison between the two groups. Your diocesan office should be able to advise you on PCCs with Friends groups that you can talk to before embarking on the process yourself. Always remember that it is the PCC that remains responsible for the building and therefore the body that applies for grants and pays the bills. The Friends are there to help generate income through events and other activities and should never be put in the position of dictating the building's priorities.

Subcommittees of the PCC

Another solution is to form a subcommittee of the PCC which is then allocated the task of raising the funds to maintain the building. The downside of this is that a subcommittee of

Friends groups can organise fundraising events.

the PCC, unlike a separate charity, might be viewed by grant-making bodies as primarily a mission and ministry organisation rather than one to safeguard the fabric of the building.

See Chapter 9 for sources of more information on Friends groups and funding.

VAT

The payment of VAT on repairs has long been an issue for places of worship. Decisions on goods and services attracting VAT, the levels of tax, and what is eligible for zero rating are controlled by the European Union but the UK Government introduced a form of relief with its Listed Places of Worship Grant Scheme (www.lpwscheme.org.uk).

Many think this is a straightforward refund of VAT paid on work to listed churches but technically it is a sum equivalent to the VAT that is refunded. The LPWGS is a helpful source of funding, albeit only for listed churches, but the total bill, including VAT, must be paid to the contractor before you can claim the grant, which means you'll need to ensure your cash flow is sufficient.

The Government has broadened and narrowed the remit of the scheme in equal measure over its lifetime and its future is not absolutely guaranteed. At the time of writing, it remains a useful resource and I urge you to fight for its retention if you hear of its possible demise.

Be neighbourly

We can be lazy about sharing good practice, perhaps because we are over-modest about our successes. Neighbouring churches might benefit hugely from our experience and vice versa so don't be shy about sharing.

Other sources of funding

County Trusts

Many counties have historic churches trusts raising money through the annual sponsored Ride 'n' Stride event. As well as offering grants to churches and chapels within their area they may also be able to offer advice on other sources of funding.

National Churches Trust

The NCT is able to assist churches with larger repair projects (currently over £100,000) and community-based projects (over £25,000). The Trust has information on managing projects and other funders on its excellent website (www.nationalchurchestrust.org).

All Churches Trust

Grants are available for churches, religious charities and UK heritage-based charities (www.allchurchestrust.co.uk).

Landfill Communities Fund

Tax on landfill can be directed towards the Landfill Communities Fund which has a number of objectives. Object E is: The repair, maintenance or restoration of a building or structure which is a place of religious worship or of historic or architectural interest (www.entrust.org.uk/landfill-community-fund).

Note 1.

If there is a moral objection you can apply to English Heritage for a grant from its Historic Buildings, Monuments and Designed Landscapes fund. The application should describe the objection and be supported by a copy of the resolution from the minutes of the meeting. However, they can only consider applications for grade 1 and grade 2 churches and can fund only urgent repair projects. Any application would be considered alongside other applications for funding. An early, pre-application discussion with your local EH office is recommended. More information can be found at www.english-heritage.org.uk/publications/historic-buildings-monuments-and-designed-landscapes/

Note 2.

I recall a church that needed repairs to its south porch. Various fundraising activities were planned and everyone was informed through the publicity material that these were for the purpose of raising money to repair the south porch. The PCC was also successful in attracting grants. Once the repair was completed and the porch made weatherproof, the PCC still had a sizeable sum in their south porch repair fund. As this was the basis on which the money was raised it could not be legally used for anything else. It would have been better if the money had been raised for the fabric of the church. This could have legitimately included the porch and any surplus could have been used on other repairs.

Note 3.

I have been secretary to a grant-making trust. It is important to complete the application form properly. If, for example, there is a space for you to describe the planned work, don't write 'Please see attached schedule'. Take time to make the reader's job as easy as possible and provide all the information clearly and concisely.

Chapter 8

Who's Who?

Individuals

Archdeacon

A senior clergy person with responsibility for clergy and legal procedures in their archdeaconry. A member of the DAC and an officer of the consistory court able to issue licences for temporary re-ordering and to authorise minor works to churches under the current system (Archdeacon's Faculty) and the new system (List B).

Architect/Surveyor

One of the PCC's key professional advisers. Every five years each church has a survey undertaken by an architect or surveyor from your DAC's list of professionals with proven experience in church buildings. It is recommended the same person oversees work between inspections so as to build up both a knowledge of the building and a rapport with the wardens and PCC. For Heritage Lottery Fund grant-aided work an architect must be listed on the Architects Accredited in Building Conservation (AABC) register at category A or the Royal Institute of British Architects' (RIBA) conservation register at Specialist Conservation Architect level. Surveyors need to be listed on the Royal Institution of Chartered Surveyors' (RICS) Building Conservation Accreditation register.

Chancellor

A barrister or judge appointed by the bishop to be the head legal officer of the diocese. The chancellor presides over the diocese's consistory court and grants (or refuses) faculties following advice from his advisory committee (the DAC).

Churchwarden

An officer of the Parochial Church Council elected at the annual parochial church meeting. Each parish church should have two and their appointment and work is governed by the Churchwardens Measure 2001.

Diocesan Advisory Committee / DAC Secretary

The DAC is a statutory committee in each diocese advising the chancellor on faculty applications. The DAC secretary is usually a member of the diocesan office staff and should be the first point of contact for PCCs.

Diocesan Registrar

A legal officer who advises the bishop and PCCs on legal matters. The registrar acts for the chancellor in processing the paperwork for faculties.

Petitioners

The individuals applying for a faculty. Normally, but not necessarily, the priest and the two churchwardens. They need to sign the petition form and have their names on the public notices. The faculty form asks for a PCC contact and, although it could be one of the petitioners, this may be someone else such as a fabric officer or PCC secretary.

Occasionally, a private individual or an organisation is the petitioner.

Rural/Area Dean

A clergy person appointed by the bishop with oversight of a deanery. Should sign headstone applications when a benefice is without a priest.

Organisations

Bat Conservation Trust

The BCT is an umbrella trust for a variety of bat conservation groups. They administer Natural England's Bat Helpline: www.bats.org.uk, 0845 1300 228, enquiries@bats.org.uk

Church Buildings Council

The CBC is the Church of England's national statutory body advising chancellors, DACs and PCCs on works to church buildings. It is responsible for the ChurchCare website and is a vehicle for the distribution of grants for the care of churches and their fittings. The CBC may attend site visits with the DAC when major alterations or re-orderings are planned. www.churchcare.co.uk, 0207 898 1863, churchcare@churchofengland.org

Commonwealth War Graves Commission

The CWGC maintains cemeteries and memorials across 153 countries for the 1.7 million members of the Commonwealth who died in the two world wars. Many memorials are within churchyards. Must be consulted if any of their memorials are likely to be affected by work in a churchyard. www.chgc.org, 01628 634221.

English Heritage/Historic England

At the time of writing, English Heritage is the UK Government's heritage specialist organisation. While its head office is in London, casework is handled at nine regional offices where the historic buildings inspectors are based. The inspectors are likely to be involved with church buildings through attending site visits and corresponding with PCCs, PCC architects and DACs. Each DAC has a member representing English Heritage, although this does not remove the need to consult directly if necessary.

Please note: English Heritage separates into two organisations on 1 April 2015. A new charity, English Heritage, will maintain the historic sites, known as the National Heritage Collection. A new body, Historic England, will be responsible for preserving England's wider historic environment and will be the group involved with church buildings. www.historicengland.org.uk, 020 7973 3700.

Environment Agency

The Environment Agency is a public body sponsored by the Department of the Environment, Food and Rural Affairs. Permission needs to be sought from the EA if planning a trench-arch drainage system. www.gov.uk/government/organisations/environment-agency, 03708 506 506, enquiries@environment-agency.gov.uk

Food Standards Agency

The Food Standards Agency is responsible for food safety and food hygiene across the UK. www.food.gov.uk, 020 7276 8829, helpline@foodstandards.gsi.gov.uk

Heritage Lottery Fund

The HLF is a grant body able to assist with funding church repairs and improvements. It will require PCCs to introduce or broaden community involvement with the project and building. The HLF is interested in the outcome of the project – focusing on the difference the grant will make to the heritage, the people involved and the wider community. The HLF runs the Grants for Places of Worship (GPOW) for urgent structural repairs to listed churches. PCCs are also able to apply for other strands of Lottery funding. These will also use potential outcomes as important ways of judging the project but may have different requirements for match-funding, application processes and deadline. There are 12 local offices across the UK.

www.hlf.org.uk, Head office: 020 7591 6000,
Grant enquiries: 020 7591 6042, enquire@hlf.org.uk

Natural England

NE is the Government's adviser on the natural environment. Its permission is necessary, via the issuing of a licence, when repairs to churches may affect a bat roost. It is illegal to deliberately harm or disturb bats or their roosts and PCCs should consult their professional adviser or ring the Bat Advice Line on 0845 1300 228 if in any doubt.

www.gov.uk/government/organisations/natural-england, 0300 060 6000, enquiries@naturalengland.org.uk

Royal British Legion

It is advisable to consult the RBL in connection with any work to war memorials both inside a church or in the churchyard. This may include the memorial's cleaning, re-cutting and especially the adding of names. The Legion is organised in regions each split into areas.

www.britishlegion.org.uk, 0808 802 8080.

Shrinking the Footprint

Shrinking the Footprint is part of ChurchCare with the emphasis on providing tools to reduce the carbon footprint of the Church of England. The website has information for PCCs including case studies, contacts for grants and worship resources.
www.churchcare.co.uk/shrinking-the-footprint,
0207 898 1863, churchcare@churchofengland.org

The National Amenity Societies

These are societies in the secular sector, that must be notified by the local planning authority of any application to demolish all or part of a listed building. The faculty jurisdiction system aims to be as robust as the secular system and therefore these groups should be involved as the need arises. Your DAC secretary or registrar will advise as to who should be consulted and at what stage.

Ancient Monuments Society

The AMS was founded 'for the study and conservation of ancient monuments, historic buildings and fine old craftsmanship'. Its partner organisation, the Friends of Friendless Churches, cares for a number of churches that have closed for public worship.
www.ancientmonumentssociety.org.uk, 020 7236 3934,
office@ancientmonumentssociety.org.uk

Council for British Archaeology

The CBA's interest is above ground as well as below and is not simply restricted to historic sites and materials.
www.archaeologyuk.org, 01904 671 417,
webenquiry@archaeologyUK.org

Society for the Protection of Ancient Buildings

The SPAB's interest is in buildings and their contents prior to 1700 so is potentially involved in many church and cathedral building projects. The SPAB developed the Faith in Maintenance initiative encouraging PCCs to consider routine maintenance as essential work. Building on the success of FiM, the SPAB is running Maintenance Co-Operative Projects aimed at creating active local groups confident in carrying out preventative maintenance on church buildings. www.spab.org.uk, 020 7377 1644, casework@spab.org.uk

Georgian Group

The Group has an interest in buildings dating from 1700 to 1837 and may need to be consulted over changes to churches which are likely to affect Georgian architecture, fittings or furniture.
www.georgiangroup.org.uk, 020 7529 8920,
info@georgiangroup.org.uk

Victorian Society

The Society's focus is on buildings and contents from the Victorian and Edwardian eras. It also has an interest in older churches where Victorian restorers modified the building or introduced furniture and fittings. The Society has a full-time churches officer and, like all the amenity societies, it is wise to consult early when works will affect churches or furniture from this period.
www.victoriansociety.org.uk, 020 8994 1019,
admin@victoriansociety.org.uk

The Twentieth Century Society

The Society picks up the baton from the Victorian Society taking an interest in the architecture and design of buildings

CARING FOR YOUR CHURCH BUILDING

from 1914. A number of churches will fall into this category and the Society should be consulted where appropriate. Your DAC secretary or registrar should be able to advise when this is necessary.
www.c20society.org.uk, 020 7250 3857, caseworker@c20society.org.uk

Common abbreviations:

AABC: Architect Accredited in Building Conservation

BCT: Bat Conservation Trust

BIOS: British Institute of Organ Studies

CBC: Church Buildings Council

CMP: Conservation Management Plan

CWGC: Commonwealth War Graves Commission

DAC: Diocesan Advisory Committee (for the Care of Churches)

DBF: Diocesan Board of Finance

DCMS: Department for Culture, Media and Sport

EASA: Ecclesiastical Architects and Surveyors Association

ECA: Electrical Contractors Association

EH: English Heritage

FiM: Faith in Maintenance – the SPAB's maintenance initiative

GPOW: (Heritage Lottery Fund's) Grants for Places of Worship

HE: Historic England

HLF: Heritage Lottery Fund

IET: Institution of Engineering and Technology

LED: Light Emitting Diode

LPWGS: Listed Places of Worship Grant Scheme

MICC: Mineral-insulated copper-clad – a type of cable

MoJ: Ministry of Justice

NADFAS: National Association of Decorative and Fine Arts Societies

NAPIT: National Association of Professional Inspectors and Testers

NICEIC: National Inspection Council for Electrical Installation Contracting

PAT: Portable Appliance Testing

PCC: Parochial Church Council

PIR: Passive Infra-Red

PV: Photo-Voltaic panels or cells.

QIR: Quinquennial Inspection Report

RBL: Royal British Legion

RIBA: Royal Institute of British Architects

RICS: Royal Institution of Chartered Surveyors

SoN: Statement of Needs

SoS: Statement of Significance

SPAB: Society for the Protection of Ancient Buildings

TPO: Tree Preservation Order

Chapter 9

Further Reading/Information

Books

A Basic Church Dictionary by Tony Meakin.
Canterbury Press 1-85311-259-3
A very handy dictionary covering a range of Church-based subjects.

Church Architecture: A Glossary of Terms by Mark Child.
Shire Publications Ltd 978-0852633281
Sorts out the reticulated tracery from the perpendicular. An ideal reference book for building terms.

Church Extensions and Adaptations.
Church House Publishing 978-0715175972
A guide for PCCs considering extending or adapting their church.

Church Floors and Floor Coverings by Daryl Fowler.
Church House Publishing 978-0715175637
Offers advice on how to care for old and new floors and to assist in the selection of new floor finishes.

The Churchyards Handbook.
Church House Publishing 0-7151-7583-1
An excellent book covering the whole subject of churchyards whether open or closed.

The Conservation and Repair of Bells and Bellframes.
Church House Publishing 978-0715142509

Obtaining a balance between meeting the demands of ringers and conservation practices can be difficult. This book offers advice and guidance on how that balance can be found. Revised and updated in 2011 and available as a free download from churchcare.co.uk

Fire Safety and Security in Places of Worship.
HIS BRE Press 978-1-84806-063-0
A useful book covering the reduction of risk from fire and other dangers.

A Fragile Inheritance – the Care of Stained Glass and Historic Glazing by Sebastian Strobl and Sarah Brown.
Church House Publishing 978-0715176009
Contains guidance on the deterioration of glass, its conservation and future care.

Fundraising for Your Church Building.
Church House Publishing 978-0715176016
Advice from the Church Buildings Council for raising funds towards building projects.

Handle with Prayer: A church cleaner's notebook by Graham Jeffery. Church House Publishing 978-0715175620
A practical and humorous guide to cleaning the church.

Heating Your Church by William Bordass and Colin Bemrose.
Church House Publishing 978-071517570X
Published in 1996 it contains helpful advice but doesn't include more modern forms of heating.

Historic Organ Conservation by Dominic Gwynn.
Church House Publishing 978-0715175927

A practical guide covering a wide range of subjects including the availability of advice and grants.

How to Read a Church by Richard Taylor.
Rider 184413053-3
A clear explanation of the use and meaning behind church architecture, fixtures and fittings.

A Little History of the English Country Church by Roy Strong.
Jonathan Cape 978-0-224-07522-0
A fascinating and very readable history of the country church.

Making Church Buildings Work by Maggie Durran.
Canterbury Press 1-85311-597-5
A practical guide covering church building projects from planning to implementation.

Open for You by Paul Bond.
Canterbury Press 1-85311-714-5
How to open your church to visitors, pilgrims and the wider community.

Practical Church Management by James Behrens.
Gracewing 0-85244-471-0
Covers a wide range of subjects for PCCs and other congregations. First published in 1998.

Re-pitching the Tent: Re-ordering Your Church Building for Worship and Mission by Richard Giles.
Canterbury Press 978-1853112454
The seminal book on liturgical re-ordering.

Responsible Care for Churchyards.
Church House Publishing 978-0715175644
A short booklet published in 1993 but still relevant today.

Revealing the Past, Informing the Future: A Guide to Archaeology for Parishes by Joseph Elders.
Church House Publishing 978-0715176030
An easy to read and invaluable guide for PCCs. Archaeology is above ground as well as below and this book offers advice to everyone looking after a parish church.

Sounds Good by John Norman and Jim Berrow.
Church House Publishing 978-0715175941
A guide to church organs for incumbents, churchwardens and PCCs.

A Stitch in Time.
Church House Publishing 978-0715175958
Guidance on how to care for church textiles.

Stonework: Maintenance and Surface Repair.
Church House Publishing 978-0715175828
Recognised as a classic work on repairs to stonework.

The Turret Clock Keeper's Handbook by Chris McKay.
CreateSpace Independent Publishing Platform
978-1492317708
A revised edition of this excellent manual for those caring for turret clocks.

Widening the Eye of the Needle by John Penton.
Church House Publishing 978-0-7151-4061-1

An invaluable book covering the subject of access to church buildings, including a model access audit.

Wiring of Churches by the Revd A G Sage.
Church House Publishing 978-0715175718
Published in 1997 this contains information still current today.

Websites

Advice

British Institute of Organ Studies

Valuable source of information on church pipe organs: www.bios.org.uk

British Listed Buildings

Website containing the listing for every listed building in the UK. Useful to check the grade of your church or chapel and a basis for any Statement of Significance: www.britishlistedbuildings.co.uk

Caring for God's Acre

Resources for looking after churchyards: www.caringforgodsacre.org.uk

Church Bells

The Central Council of Church Bell Ringers with contacts for advice and publications: www.cccbr.org.uk

Churchcare

Comprehensive and up-to-date advice on all aspects of looking after church buildings: www.churchcare.co.uk

Conservation Register

Information on finding a conservator and how to look after valuable contents: www.conservationregister.com

Council for British Archaeology

Advice on archaeology: new.archaeologyuk.org

Ecclesiastical

Church building insurer with guidance notes on a range of subjects: www.ecclesiastical.com/churchmatters

Georgian Group

Information on the amenity society responsible for Georgian architecture and fittings: www.georgiangroup.org.uk

Historic England

Advice on heritage crime, fundraising and caring for places of worship: www.historicengland.org.uk

Parish Resources

Church of England site offering advice on all aspects of running a PCC including church buildings, fundraising and Friends organisations: www.parishresources.org.uk

Shrinking the Footprint

Church of England site on reducing the Church's carbon footprint. Help and advice on forms of power generation, grants and good practice:
www.churchcare.co.uk/shrinking-the-footprint

Society for the Protection of Ancient Buildings

Advice on looking after old buildings and policy statements on extensions to churches: www.spab.org.uk

The 20th Century Society

Campaign group for buildings and fittings from the 20th century: www.c20society.org.uk

Victorian Society

Information on this campaign group for Victorian and Edwardian architecture and fittings: www.victoriansociety.org.uk

Funding

All Churches Trust

Grants are available for churches, religious charities and UK heritage-based charities: www.allchurchestrust.co.uk

Funds for Historic Buildings

Website with funding advice with funders' database for all historic buildings including churches: www.ffhb.org.uk

Heritage Lottery Fund

Advice on grants for places of worship and community projects: www.hlf.org.uk

Listed Places of Worship Grant Scheme

The Government's scheme to refund a sum equivalent to the VAT paid on listed church repairs and improvements: www.lpwscheme.org.uk

National Churches Trust

Grant-making trust with other useful advice:
www.nationalchurchestrust.org

Parish Resources

Church of England site offering advice on all aspects of running a PCC including church buildings, fundraising and Friends organisations: www.parishresources.org.uk

Other denominations

The Baptist Union of Great Britain and the Baptist Union of Wales Central information on building issues for Baptist places of worship:
www.baptist.org.uk/Groups/220867/Listed_Buildings

Methodist Church

Central information on building issues for Methodist places of worship:
www.methodist.org.uk/ministers-and-office-holders/property

Methodist Chapel Aid

Offers loans to Trustees of Christian churches at competitive rates of interest: www.methodistchapel.co.uk

Roman Catholic Church

Information on local building advice is held at diocesan level.

United Reformed Church

Central information on building issues for URC places of worship:
www.urc.org.uk/plato-property-handbook1/613-plato-property-handbook

Church in Wales

Information on church buildings at:
www.churchinwales.org.uk/structure/representative-body/
church-heritage-and-conservation-resources

Church of Scotland

The central Church Art and Architecture Committee offers
advice on renovations, alterations and re-ordering schemes:
www.churchofscotland.org.uk/about_us/councils_committees_
and_departments/committees/church-art-and-architecture-
committee

Appendix A

Church Buildings Council's
Flow Chart of Faculty Application
(incorporating changes to the system taking effect in 2015/16)

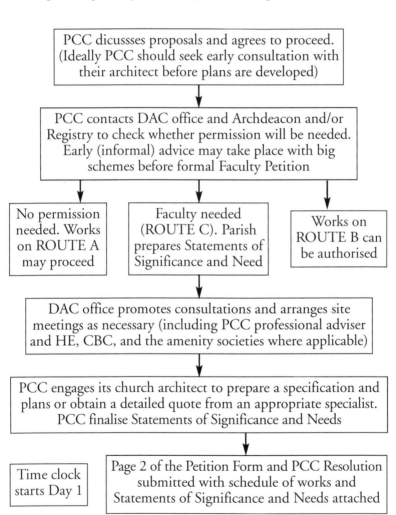

PCC dicussses proposals and agrees to proceed. (Ideally PCC should seek early consultation with their architect before plans are developed)

PCC contacts DAC office and Archdeacon and/or Registry to check whether permission will be needed. Early (informal) advice may take place with big schemes before formal Faculty Petition

No permission needed. Works on ROUTE A may proceed

Faculty needed (ROUTE C). Parish prepares Statements of Significance and Need

Works on ROUTE B can be authorised

DAC office promotes consultations and arranges site meetings as necessary (including PCC professional adviser and HE, CBC, and the amenity societies where applicable)

PCC engages its church architect to prepare a specification and plans or obtain a detailed quote from an appropriate specialist. PCC finalise Statements of Significance and Needs

Time clock starts Day 1

Page 2 of the Petition Form and PCC Resolution submitted with schedule of works and Statements of Significance and Needs attached

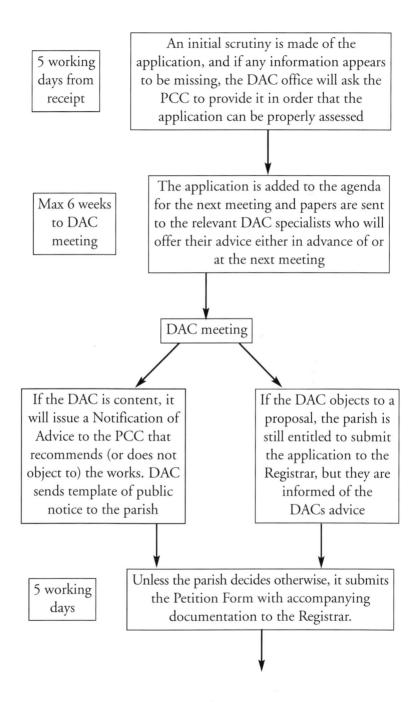

5 working days from receipt

An initial scrutiny is made of the application, and if any information appears to be missing, the DAC office will ask the PCC to provide it in order that the application can be properly assessed

Max 6 weeks to DAC meeting

The application is added to the agenda for the next meeting and papers are sent to the relevant DAC specialists who will offer their advice either in advance of or at the next meeting

DAC meeting

If the DAC is content, it will issue a Notification of Advice to the PCC that recommends (or does not object to) the works. DAC sends template of public notice to the parish

If the DAC objects to a proposal, the parish is still entitled to submit the application to the Registrar, but they are informed of the DACs advice

5 working days

Unless the parish decides otherwise, it submits the Petition Form with accompanying documentation to the Registrar.

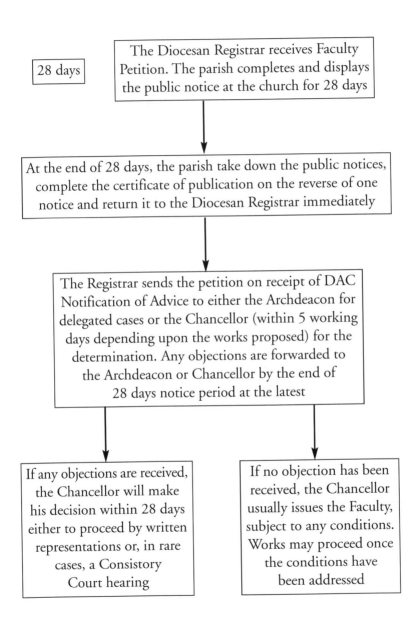

28 days

The Diocesan Registrar receives Faculty Petition. The parish completes and displays the public notice at the church for 28 days

At the end of 28 days, the parish take down the public notices, complete the certificate of publication on the reverse of one notice and return it to the Diocesan Registrar immediately

The Registrar sends the petition on receipt of DAC Notification of Advice to either the Archdeacon for delegated cases or the Chancellor (within 5 working days depending upon the works proposed) for the determination. Any objections are forwarded to the Archdeacon or Chancellor by the end of 28 days notice period at the latest

If any objections are received, the Chancellor will make his decision within 28 days either to proceed by written representations or, in rare cases, a Consistory Court hearing

If no objection has been received, the Chancellor usually issues the Faculty, subject to any conditions. Works may proceed once the conditions have been addressed

Appendix B

Church Buildings Council's guidance notes on Statements of Significance and Statements of Needs

These should be used for all projects other than very complex ones. For major complex projects an expanded version of this form is likely to be more appropriate. The Council would strongly urge that these documents are prepared at an early stage of the faculty process so as to help inform decisions and identify areas of conflict. A word version of the templates in this document is available on the ChurchCare website at http://www.churchcare.co.uk/churches/guidance-advice/statements-of-significance-need

Statement of Significance

The Faculty Jurisdiction Rules 2013 define a Statement of Significance as 'a document which describes the significance of the church or other building in terms of its special architectural and historic interest (including any contribution made by its setting) and any significant features of artistic or archaeological interest that the church or other building has so as to enable the potential impact of the proposals on its significance, and on any such features, to be understood'.

A Statement of Significance is an important tool to help everyone understand the significance of the church building and its fabric and fittings.

It is a useful resource for anyone with responsibility for your church's fabric and encourages good stewardship of your heritage building.

It should be prepared independently of any Faculty application, and ideally reviewed annually so that any recently obtained historical material or changes, such as an extension or re-ordering, can be incorporated, and a copy should be given to the Church Architect to include in his/her Quinquennial Inspection Report.

A Statement of Significance should accompany every faculty application that involves making changes to a listed church. It will help those in the Faculty system advise you and assess your plans for change.

This guidance includes a template to help you to write your Statement of Significance. It should include a ground plan and map of the local area and at least two photographs, normally one of the exterior, one of the interior. The notes in the boxes will guide you as to the sort of things to include.

In assessing significance you may wish to use the following customary terminology:

High – important at national to international levels.

Moderate-High – important at regional or sometimes higher.

Moderate – usually of local value but of regional significance for group or other value (e.g. vernacular architecture).

Low-Moderate – of local value.

Low – adds little or nothing to the value of a site or detracts from it.

Statement of Needs

The Faculty Jurisdiction Rules 2013 define a Statement of Needs as 'a document setting out the justification for the proposals' and stipulates that 'If proposals are likely to result in harm to the significance of the church or other building as a building of special architectural or historic interest, the document setting out the justification for the proposals must set out the basis on which it is said that the proposals would result in public benefit that outweighs that harm'.

A Statement of Needs should be a document which serves both the parish and those involved in the faculty process. It should be a tool for the parish, enabling the PCC to focus its vision and agree on what it seeks to achieve. For others, such as the DAC, CBC and Historic England it serves to provide easily accessible information to help assess the scheme which is being proposed for a faculty.

Statements of Needs are the parish's opportunity to explain, justify and rationalise the proposals to all interested parties.

Consider that some people will not have the opportunity to visit the church and will need to base opinions on the information you provide in these supporting statements.

Bearing this in mind, you are strongly encouraged to ensure that the Statement is factual, informative, clear and concise.

Try not to be emotive or over-dramatic. The facts of the situation should speak clearly for themselves.

Basic facts about the project

Statements of Significance and Needs must be accompanied by the Standard Information form 1A which will contain the basic facts about the project.

Statement of Significance

Section 1: Brief history and description of the church building(s), contents, churchyard and setting.

Section 2: The significance of the church (including its contents and churchyard) in terms of:

i) Its special architectural and historical interest

ii) Any significant features of artistic or archaeological interest

Please state if you have taken expert advice to help you define the significance, and from whom.

Section 3: Assessment of the impact of the proposals on the significance defined in Section 2.

Statement of Needs

Section 1: General information

This should provide an overview of the parish and the current use of the building.

Section 2: What do you need?

Briefly explain your needs (not your proposals). Append any brief for your architect.

Section 3: The proposals

Set out what you are proposing to do in order to meet the needs set out in section 2.

Section 4: Why do you need it and why do you need it now?

Justify your proposals by explaining why you can't meet your needs without making changes. Also include anything which may have prompted the proposals.

Section 5: Justification

If the proposals are likely to harm the significance outlined in the Statement of significance, explain how the proposals would result in public benefits which outweigh such harm (public benefits include matters such as liturgical freedom, pastoral well-being and putting the church to viable uses that are consistent with its role as a place of worship and mission).

Statement of Significance – Guidance on Completion

Use the following guidance and key questions to help you complete the form.

Section 1: Brief history and description of the church building(s), contents, churchyard and setting

Church Building(s)

What is the history of the church; when was a church first established on the site and how has it changed over time; who are the architects, artists and other craftsmen who have been involved; have there been any significant benefactors and has this affected the choice of architect/artist or the incorporation of any monuments in the church? How does work carried out on the church link to international, national, regional or local architectural and artistic movements? What is its plan form, spatial quality, building materials used? How is it lit and heated? What is the theological 'message' communicated by the exterior and interior of the church? Are there any significant events or personalities associated with the church? Are there important memories associated with the church or churchyard?

Contents

These may include: Altar; Reredos; Pulpit; Lectern; Font; Stained glass; Wall paintings; Bells and Bell frame; Monuments; Organ; Communion plate; Registers; Pews and other woodwork; Metalwork; Communion rails; Floor finishes. Do the contents relate to any particular historical changes to the church and

How old are the pews? Who carved the ends?

do they contribute to the significance of those changes? Are any of the artists or craftsmen of international, national, regional or local importance?

It is reasonable to group these if there is a contemporary scheme which is significant as such, for example one could say a complete scheme of eighteenth-century furnishings.

Churchyard

Is the church or churchyard used by protected species or species with Biodiversity Action Plans? Are there any ancient, very prominent, rare or unusual trees? How good a habitat is the churchyard for fauna and flora?

Setting

Are there distant or near views which are valued by the congregation/wider community/visitors/experts? How do the trees contribute to the setting? What is known of the landscape design and history of the churchyard, including extensions? Are there archaeological remains? Are adjacent buildings similar, complementary or contrasting in age, style, materials or age? How are the boundary and entrances marked? Are the monuments, war memorials significant?

Section 2: The significance of the church (including its contents and churchyard) in terms of:

i) Its special architectural and historical interest

ii) Any significant features of artistic or archaeological interest

This should provide an overview of the significance of the church, and the contribution of its setting to that significance.

This should be compiled before any specific proposal has been worked up, and can be reused for each faculty application, although of course it will have to be kept up to date. Refer to the terminology in the introductory section of this guidance document to help you define significance.

Please state if you have taken expert advice to help you define the significance, and from whom.

Section 3: Assessment of the impact of the proposals on the significance defined in Section 2

Section 3 will be prepared in draft form for any pre-application consultations, and finalised to accompany a faculty application when a scheme has been worked up.

This should not be a justification of your scheme, which should be in the Statement of Needs. The level of detail provided should be proportionate to the importance of the heritage asset and sufficient to understand the impact of the proposal on the significance of the heritage asset.

Identify the parts of the church and/or churchyard which will be directly or indirectly affected by your proposal. Describe and assess the impact of your proposal on these parts, and on the whole. Impacts could include loss, alteration, obscuring, change of setting and change of use. Characterise impacts as either low, moderate or high.

Explain how you intend, where possible, to mitigate the impact of the proposed works on the significance of the parts affected and the whole.

Sources consulted

List the sources consulted. These may include:

- 'Buildings of England' series by Pevsner
- Reports by the Royal Commission on the Historical Monuments of England (RCHME), now part of Historic England
- The local history society
- The local museum
- Diocesan Record Centre
- County Record Centre
- County Biological Records Centre
- Historic Environment Record (HER), maintained by your local authority
- Victoria County History (VCH)

Statutory designations and descriptions for churchyards, churches or objects within them can be checked through your local planning authority, Historic England and Natural England (Nature Conservation significance).

Useful websites include:

- ChurchCare: http://www.churchcare.co.uk/
- Shrinking the footprint: http://www.churchcare.co.uk/shrinking-the-footprint
- Heritage Gateway: www.heritagegateway.org.uk/
- Magic: www.magic.gov.uk
- Caring for God's: Acre www.caringforgodsacre.org.uk

Statement of Needs – Guidance on completion

Use the following guidance and key questions to help you complete the form.

Section 1: General information

This should provide an overview of the parish and the current use of the building.

This may include:

How many people live in the parish/village/town?

What different types of services take place in the church each week/month and how many people attend each of the different services on average?

How many people are on the electoral roll?

What is the age profile of the congregation? What children's provision is there? On Sundays and midweek? How many children attend these activities?

Is the church normally left open during daylight hours?

What other activities happen in the church alongside prayer and worship?

What is the financial position of the church (e.g. reserves, payment of quota)? Are funds available now or have funds been applied for or are being applied for? Please state to whom applications have been made and if applications have been successful or refused.

When was the last Quinquennial report? What were the major issues which were highlighted? Are you on top of these issues? Do you have a maintenance plan?

Section 2: What do you need?

Briefly explain your needs (not your proposals). Append any brief for your architect.

You may find it helpful to divide the needs up into areas such as:

Facilities e.g. we need one accessible toilet and the ability to serve refreshments.

Space e.g. we need a meeting room to accommodate up to 25 people sitting and 40 people standing.

Access e.g. we need to provide a permanent route into the building which is accessible for wheelchairs.

Liturgy e.g. we need to make arrangements to use a nave altar.

Other e.g. we need to install a new heating system.

Section 3: The proposals

Set out what you are proposing to do in order to meet the needs set out in section 2.

Section 4: Why do you need it and why do you need it now?

Justify your proposals by explaining why you can't meet your needs without making changes. Also include anything which may have prompted the proposals.

How will this proposal help the ministry of the church?

How will it enhance the liturgical space and services?

How will it help small group work and midweek meetings?

How will it help the mission of the church?

What new groups of people will be drawn into the life of the church?

What new activities and events will be able to take place in the church?

How will it help your financial situation?

How is the proposal contributing to the need for environmental sustainability?

Describe any recent changes which have taken place which have led to the need arising, for example:

In the church congregation: rise in numbers attending, growth in particular age group such as children, introduction of new services and activities, arrival of new Vicar or church plant.

In the local area: new housing development, increase/decrease in population, major regeneration scheme, major change in infrastructure such as transport links, employment opportunities.

In the church building: deterioration of fabric, vandalism or other damage, subsidence, etc.

In the financial situation: a large bequest may have been made, there may be a pressing need to generate more money through the use of the building due to rising costs of ministry and mission.

Section 5: Justification

If the proposals are likely to harm the significance outlined in the Statement of significance, explain how the proposals would result in public benefits which outweigh such harm (public benefits include matters such as liturgical freedom, pastoral well-being and putting the church to viable uses that are consistent with its role as a place of worship and mission).

What other options to meet the need were considered? These may include: larger or smaller schemes, different designs, locating the scheme/proposal in a different part of the church building, not making a change at all, providing a management solution rather than a change in the fabric, using a different building in the wider community e.g. school, community hall, another church. What were the pros and cons of each option?

James Halsall has also contributed to:

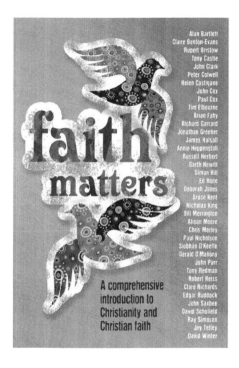

Alan Bartlett
Claire Benton-Evans
Rupert Bristow
Tony Castle
John Clark
Peter Colwell
Helen Costigane
John Cox
Paul Cox
Tim Elbourne
Brian Fahy
Richard Garrard
Jonathan Greener
James Halsall
Annie Heppenstall
Russell Herbert
Garth Hewitt
Simon Hill
Ed Hone
Deborah Jones
Bruce Kent
Nicholas King
Bill Merrington
Alison Moore
Chris Morley
Paul Nicholson
Siobhán O'Keeffe
Gerald O'Mahony
John Parr
Tony Redman
Robert Reiss
Clare Richards
Edgar Ruddock
John Saxbee
David Scholfield
Ray Simpson
Joy Tetley
David Winter

Faith Matters

A comprehensive introduction to
Christianity and Christian faith.

1501369

www.kevinmayhew.com